The Grail and the Development of Conscience

Karl König in 1962

The Grail and the Development of Conscience

St Paul and Parsifal

Karl König

Floris
Books

Karl König Archive Publication, Vol. 16
Subject: Christianity, festivals
Series editor: Richard Steel

Karl König's collected works are issued by
the Karl König Archive, Aberdeen
in co-operation with the Ita Wegman Institute
for Basic Research into Anthroposophy, Arlesheim

Appendix translated by Tascha Babbitch

First published in this form in German as *Paulus und der Gral*
by Verlag Freies Geistesleben in 2014
First published in English by Floris Books in 2016

© 2016 Trustees of the Karl König Archives

British Library CIP Data available
ISBN 978-178250-267-8
Printed in Great Britain by Bell & Bain Ltd

Contents

Introduction

Guy Cornish

Wolfram von Eschenbach begins his Parzifal poem with a complex metaphor about a magpie and warns his listeners that they will need their wits about them if they are going to grasp this 'flying metaphor'. Mobility of thinking is certainly necessary if we are to follow Wolfram's descriptions of the Grail, which is variously described as a stone, a 'thing', a cup, a platter.

Similar mobility is required if we turn to Rudolf Steiner's descriptions of the Grail.

What is the Grail? Clearly, both in the work of Wolfram and Rudolf Steiner, it is not a physical thing that can easily be described. It is rather a picture, or series of pictures if we follow the legends, which point to supersensible realities.

As an example let us turn to just one of Rudolf Steiner's descriptions. This comes at the end of his book *Esoteric Science* (or *Occult Science)*. Steiner briefly describes the stream of ancient mystery wisdom, which in the time of the development of intellectual thinking was necessarily more and more concealed (and therefore hidden or 'occult').

> 'Hidden' knowledge was now flowing, although
> imperceptibly to begin with, into people's way of thinking.
> It is self-evident that intellectual forces have continued

to reject this knowledge right into the present. But what must happen will happen in spite of any temporary rejection. Symbolically, this hidden knowledge, which is taking hold of humanity from the other side and will do so increasingly in the future, can be called 'the knowledge of the Grail'. If we learn to understand the deeper meaning of this symbol as it is presented in stories and legends, we will discover a significant image of what has been described above as the new initiation knowledge with the Christ mystery at its centre. Therefore, modern initiates can also be known as 'Grail initiates'.

The path to supersensible worlds whose first stages have been described in this book leads to the 'science of the Grail'.[1]

In essence, *Esoteric Science* is a description of the supersensible parts of the human being, the path of the soul in sleep and after death, cosmic and human evolution, and the path of initiation. All this can be seen to belong to a 'science of the Grail'.

Karl König in the lectures in this volume traces the stream of hidden or occult wisdom and shows both how this wisdom is renewed by the Grail and its importance for the present time.

Grail impulses of Rudolf Steiner in 1913

In 1913 Rudolf Steiner gave two important lecture cycles about the Grail. First, in February, *The Mysteries of the East and of Christianity,* where, among other things, Rudolf Steiner describes the importance of Parsifal for our own time, the age of the consciousness soul. Karl König refers to these lectures in 1954 when exploring the role of the Grail in the development of Europe. Then in December Steiner gave the lectures, *Christ and the Spiritual World* and *The Search for the Holy Grail.* Here, in relation to Parsifal, he shared details about how over the course of some years he went about spiritual research. König refers to this research especially in Lecture 6 (*King Arthur and the Grail*).

In September 1913 the foundation stone of the first Goetheanum was laid in Dornach. Rudolf Steiner did not want to describe this building as a temple, but in lectures about the ideals connected with the building he placed the Goetheanum in a series together with a Greek temple and a Gothic cathedral, showing it clearly to be an example of sacred architecture. I believe that we can describe the first Goetheanum as a modern Grail temple if we make clear that it was open for all humankind. Like the Christmas message of the angels it was a gift for all who are of good will. Rudolf Steiner emphasised that the forms of the building could not and should not be intellectually interpreted and did not have a symbolic or allegorical sense, but were a direct artistic expression of spiritual truths.

Until the end of the Dark Age (Kali Yuga) in 1899/1900 it was necessary that the temples guarded and kept their knowledge secret from the uninitiated. At the beginning of a new light age Rudolf Steiner broke with this tradition of secrecy and revealed more and more esoteric wisdom. Goethe, whose soul was open to the dawning of a new spiritual era, expressed in his fairy tale *The Green Snake and the Beautiful Lily* many of the truths later expressed in anthroposophy. In this fairy tale an underground temple rises up and at the end of the story stands fully revealed beside a wide bridge on which humanity can cross the river in both directions. What Goethe wrote as a poetic image was realised by Rudolf Steiner in the first Goetheanum.

Karl König's deepest striving was to make a contribution to the building of the new temple, a modern Grail temple accessible to all. On this path he sought and found others who were willing to unite in a spiritual community and to work for the needs of our time. At the latest in 1945 as the Second World War was ending, König made it clear that he intended to connect to the Grail stream and to the social impulse behind the building of the first Goetheanum. In July and August 1945 he organised two conferences on the Christian element in anthroposophical medicine, and about Goethe and the first Goetheanum, though already in 1939 in his opening address in Kirkton House, where the community began in Scotland, König pointed to the wider historical background that they wanted to connect to:

> It is significant that we are here in Scotland where the great Hibernian mysteries were active ... Rudolf Steiner spoke about two streams of Christianity. One stream, connected with the forces of the blood came from the East. This began with the disciples and spread westwards through Europe as the Grail stream of the Christ. The second stream, whose origin was in Ireland, Scotland and Cornwall, flowed to the Continent, where in Central Europe, it united with the other stream ... We should understand this rightly. We should not consider ourselves as the carriers of a mission, but we should attempt to bring about a meeting between the English Spirit and the Spirit of Central Europe ... and perhaps the Spirit will allow us to make a contribution.[2]

A modern seeker of the Grail

Karl König was a man of many talents. He was among other things, a physician, lecturer and founder of the Camphill movement, as well as being a pioneer in the fields of anthroposophical curative education and social therapy. He also had a gift both for creating and changing social forms. These outer activities were based on an intense inner life and research on the basis of anthroposophy.

As a young man, long before his encounter with anthroposophy, König was deeply concerned with the theme of the Grail. In his diary in 1920 – he was seventeen years old – he wrote:

> *Palestrina* and *The Woman Without a Shadow* are the greatest works after *Parsifal* and *Tristan*. I have heard

Tristan once more. It is one of the greatest works of humanity, as is *Parsifal*. There is such depth and divinity in both these works.

Before his twentieth birthday he wrote a story which has a largely autobiographical character, stating:

> Strength you have, Lucifer. Strength of feeling and intoxicating beauty. But this force must be transformed into knowledge. Into the stone which fell from his crown flowed the holy blood of Christ. The stone began to glow and shine. So must our soul be filled with the Spirit of Christ and must shine and become a Grail.

Much later, stimulated through inner experiences, he discovered that his own name pointed to a Grail motif. Here is an excerpt from his diary from March 14, 1945, that one could take humourously, but which has an underlying seriousness:

> Tilla came early to my bedside and told her dream: She was in a large house and climbed to the tower. There she saw the sky filled with stars and between the stars silver stripes. She asked Thomas to call the friends together and to tell them to look at this sight. She then went down and came into a room. I was standing at a table and preparing a fish. She thought I was taking out the gall bladder in order to heal blind people. I am deeply moved by the dream because, like the conversation yesterday with C., it points to the Grail. Then it occurred to me that the maiden name of my mother was Fischer. So together my father and mother have given me the name 'Fisher-King'.

Often, as in these lectures, König presented the results of his research to the co-workers in Camphill, Scotland. The lectures delve into the past, especially into the esoteric streams of Christianity. For König such studies were not abstract intellectual exercises but were undertaken in order to deepen our understanding of the present. If one seeks for an inner motif underlying König's life and work one could call him a modern day seeker of the Grail.

This means, as we have seen in the quotation from Rudolf Steiner's *Esoteric Science,* that the events to which the images of the Grail stories refer belong as much to the present as to the past. It is one of the important revelations of Rudolf Steiner that a renewed crucifixion of Christ took place in the spiritual world during the nineteenth century due to the materialistic thinking of human beings. A renewal of the forces of resurrection began in the twentieth century. This calls for our active participation through understanding. Knowledge of the Christian forces of resurrection and renewal may equally well be called 'the science of the Grail' or 'anthroposophy'.

It was this ideal that Karl König served in both inner and outer life. A wonderful expression of this can be found in one of the 'early images' he gave, written down by Anke Weihs in the early days of Camphill:

> There is a knighthood of the twentieth century, whose
> members do not ride through the darkness of physical
> forests as of old, but through forests of darkened minds.
> They are armed with a spiritual armour, and an inner
> sun makes them radiant. Out of them shines healing –
> healing that flows from a knowing of the image of man
> as a spiritual being. They must create inner order, inner
> justice, peace and conviction in the darkness of our time.[3]

Let there be fired from the east
what is formed in the west ...

There is a legend about Joseph of Arimathea which relates that he was told by an angel to carry the Grail to the West, and that he should keep travelling until he came to a place in which his staff, when stuck in the ground, would flower. There Joseph should found the community of the Grail. He and his little band journeyed through France and only when they reached Glastonbury in the south-west of England did the wonder of the sprouting staff occur. Joseph settled in the area together with his sister and her husband Bron and their twelve children.

We can cast light on this legend through a lecture that Rudolf Steiner gave in Torquay in 1924. He describes the Grail stream as coming from the East and carrying awareness of the being of Christ. This meets with a remnant of the wisdom of the Hibernian or Celtic mysteries in the West. The initiates of these mysteries experienced the mighty being of the sun as the creator of the cosmos and were also aware that this being would one day incarnate in a human form.

In the legend, the twelve sons of Bron indicate the cosmic principle of the zodiac which was also expressed in the Round Table of King Arthur. This wisdom united with the knowledge of the being of Christ in order to form the Grail community.

Can we see a similar gesture in the destiny of Karl König and the small group who founded Camphill? They came from Central Europe carrying the impulse to found a community based on anthroposophy, and were led by destiny to Camphill House in the north of Scotland. Only later did they discover the connection of this area to the Knights Templar. An inner impulse takes on form and works into the world in the west. Was this chance or the working of destiny?

Rudolf Steiner connects the Grail with the stream of esoteric Christianity deriving from Lazarus-John. Why does Karl König place so much emphasis on St Paul? In the third lecture (on the sixth century) he quotes Rudolf Steiner as saying that the true follower of John is Paul because both were initiated by the Christ.

The connection between Paul and the Grail

König gives two possible aspects to this connection: 'One part of the mystery of the Grail is the mystery of blood'. The basis for humanity's ancient clairvoyance was the blood, but this came to an end. And Paul through his initiation, through the experience at Damascus, learns something entirely new:

> It was altogether due to the disappearance of the mystical powers of this very special fluid that the mystery of blood could dawn within the human soul. Paul was the one who was able to point this out (p. 74).

A second aspect appears through considering Rudolf Steiner's interpretation of the legend that the Grail was formed from a jewel which fell from Lucifer's crown: 'this jewel is nothing else than the full power of the human ego' and König continues:

> What do we really mean if we try to grapple with this image that the human self or ego is the stone formed into a cup, which received the blood of Christ? We must immediately think of Paul and of his experience, 'Not I, but the Christ in me.' (p. 76).

Another possible reason for the emphasis on Paul may be that he was a forerunner of the consciousness soul and therefore his experiences are particularly relevant to the present time. Although König does not say this directly, the whole tenor of the lectures makes clear the relevance and importance of Paul's contribution to an understanding of the Grail in our time.

The lectures given in 1962

These lectures describe the origin of the stream of esoteric Christianity, which came about through the meeting of St Paul and Dionysius the Areopagite. It is probable that they only met once, so how was Dionysius able to immediately recognise the importance of what Paul brought?

He was an initiate of the Eleusinian mysteries which developed out of the Mithraic mysteries. König describes these and the primeval wisdom which they preserved. This was renewed and rejuvenated through the meeting with Christianity in the esoteric school founded by Paul. König outlines the development of exoteric and esoteric Christianity. He connects the mysteries of bread to the cosmos, while the mysteries of wine are related to the inner nature of the human being. Images reflecting both these mysteries can be found in the Grail stories. König describes the development of memory and conscience, both historically and in the present, as a path to the Grail. A central theme running through these lectures connects Paul with Parsifal and with Rudolf Steiner, not as reincarnations of a single individuality but as carriers of an endeavour to found a new kind of community based upon individual freedom and insight into the spirit.

The lectures given in 1954

König was concerned with tracing the spiritual development of Europe and saw its quintessential task as preparing and carrying the mysteries of the Grail. This theme is touched on in the 1962 lectures but is explored in considerable detail in the lectures given in 1954. This year was a difficult one in König's biography. A few months after he gave these lectures he became severely ill and for more than a year was close to death. Through the words of these lectures something of his own destiny shines through, as does his connection with the destiny of Central Europe.

In the first of the lectures he posed the central question:

> Will Europe be able to discover her present task? The
> last two thousand years culminating in the twentieth

15

century have seen continuous attempts to build up
Europe. From a spiritual point of view, all the streams of
development flow together and raise the great question,
will Europe understand its task? What is the task? The
task is that European people learn to understand the path
to the Holy Grail. For this Europe was created. Only if
the different nations of Europe are able to understand
this, will the possibility come to grow out of the present
dilemma. (p. 106)

Using Rudolf Steiner's research, König shows how Europe
was formed out of the tension between exoteric and esoteric
Christianity. Behind the outer course of history beings of the
spiritual hierarchies are working:

World history is cosmic evolution. All that we suffer as
well as enjoy, is part of this evolution through which the
angelic and archangelic beings connected with human
beings have to go. (p. 106)

In the second lecture König describes the mystery of the
Holy Grail as 'a mystery of the human astral body,' and shows
how through gradual purification our astral body can receive
the highest spiritual existence: 'This empty chalice of our astral
body can, if willing, receive the Son of God, the highest form of
spiritual existence'. (p. 115)

König began the year 1954 with lectures on the 'Fifth Gospel'
and alongside all his other tasks held over 80 lectures before
illness forced him to withdraw from outer activity. He fully
recovered only in the spring of 1956, but he had touched on
the important theme of memory and conscience on which he
continued to work for the rest of his life. Seven years later in 1961
this theme appeared on a new level and formed a background for
the building of Camphill Hall in Scotland (also called the 'Hall
of Memory and Conscience'). König's pursuit of this theme may
well have led to his return to Central Europe in 1962. These
experiences were interwoven with König's deep connection with

Kaspar Hauser. König held lectures in Nürnberg (where Kaspar had appeared in 1828) on memory and conscience. He visited Ansbach, where Hauser died (which is also near to the birthplace of Wolfram von Eschenbach). Karl Heyer, whose book about Kaspar Hauser König reviewed in 1958, wrote:

> An inner relationship can be drawn between the renewed office of the priest-king, which was the true calling of the individuality of Kaspar Hauser, and the being of the Grail King as presented by Richard Wagner in his *Parsifal*. In a certain sense we can say that Kaspar Hauser was the 'pure fool' who knew neither his own name nor his origin.[4]

The Easter lectures of 1954 were not taken down in shorthand, so there are only incomplete notes available taken down by listeners. They are published here with the later 1962 lectures because they contain additional aspects. In the seven years between the two series of lectures on the Grail, König gave lectures about other aspects of Easter which allow us to follow his path: in 1959 he spoke about the reappearance of the Christ and the new organ of perception following the Damascus experience, and in 1960 he spoke about the Goetheanum and the Grail. It is planned to publish these lectures in future.

The present

Every age has created new versions of the Grail stories. We can think of Malory, Tennyson, Wagner and T.S. Eliot, for example. But a *knowledge* of the Grail is relatively new and was revealed for the first time by Rudolf Steiner. This work was continued by his pupils Walter Johannes Stein, Rudolf Meyer, Karl König and others. This knowledge is not primarily concerned with the medieval legends (though these are a rich source) but is orientated to the present and future, to the renewed presence of the Christ in the etheric realm. This presence enables the treasures of ancient wisdom to be rejuvenated and given a modern form accessible to our thinking.

The search for the Grail is an inner motif of destiny of an increasing number of people today. They may find much of value in this volume. Although these lectures were given over fifty years ago they have lost nothing of their relevance or originality; above all because they take up themes that Rudolf Steiner considered important, and place them in a new context. A hundred years after Rudolf Steiner's important revelations concerning the Grail it seems appropriate to make König's lectures available to a wider circle. The cultivation of the forces of memory and the new conscience appear as a modern path to the Grail.

St Paul and the Grail

Lectures held in Newton Dee, Aberdeen, 1962

1

The School of Athens

Lecture 1,
Sunday, February 4, 1962

I would like to show some slides and reproductions of pictures by Raphael in order to gain an impression of these very special pieces of art, especially of the painting known as the *School of Athens*.

I spoke about this picture during one of my lectures on conscience in connection with St Paul.[1] I mentioned it because in it Paul is shown at the very special moment when he enters Athens and meets the one who is depicted in this picture as the old man at his side, who in the Bible and in history is called Dionysius the Areopagite. That it is Paul and Dionysius is not commonly known because art historians usually describe these two figures as Aristotle and Plato, but Rudolf Steiner made it quite clear on many occasions that they are neither Aristotle nor Plato but the two personalities I have just mentioned. Of course one might ask why we should spend a whole evening on this picture, but Rudolf Steiner gave several lectures during the course of his teaching speaking only about Raphael's *School of Athens*. And certain indications in one or other of these lectures seemed to me of such importance for our study of human conscience in connection with the figure of St Paul – especially

Paul and the mysteries of the Holy Grail – that an intimate awareness of the *School of Athens* seems necessary.

This mural is to be found in the Camera della Segnatura in the Vatican in Rome, which is not a big room by any means. You can enter it from either side and you will find the *School of Athens* painted on one wall, and opposite it the picture which was later called the *Disputa*. The two face each other and it is probable that Pope Julius II, who commissioned the painting of these two pictures by Raphael, sat in front of the *Disputa* when he was writing and working. He was not praying; he was writing and scheming. As a pope he was ferocious, much more a conqueror and a knight (in fact something of a dark knight), but he was definitely not a Christian, nor was he a praying individual. So we can imagine him sitting in front of the *Disputa* when he was signing his papers, and behind him the picture known today as the *School of Athens*. Let us now look at these two pictures in order to gain a first impression, and then we will go on to ask several questions in connection with them.

First the *School of Athens* (see Plate 1 after p. 32). Here in the sky between the arches, you see open space. Everything else is enclosed, sheltered inside a building. There are walls, but walls that are interrupted, and the whole picture is perfectly symmetrical. To the right and left of the two central figures, who were always thought to be Aristotle and Plato but whom we now know to be Paul and Dionysius the Areopagite, groups of people are standing, all of them Greek scientists and philosophers. Rudolf Steiner never approved of attempts to identify these philosophers, although one can more or less make out Socrates, Archimedes and others, but Rudolf Steiner did not like this naming. He said – as do art historians – that in the various groups Raphael depicted the seven liberal arts; astronomy, mathematics, geometry, dialectics, and so on. It is not necessary to describe this in detail. More important are the two central figures – a younger and an older one. The younger one, Paul, is pointing forwards, the older one, Dionysius, is pointing upwards; apart from a few people in their immediate surroundings who are looking at them, the others appear to be completely oblivious of them. They are engrossed in their own writing, discussion, study, philosophy, and so on. A wonderful harmony streams through the picture, as from all Raphael's pictures, and something speaks out of it which we can call the true revelation of Greece.

The *Disputa* (Plate 2) is a very different picture from the *School of Athens* in which the pillars and arches completely surround and enclose the people. In the *Disputa* everything is open. In the centre stands an altar on which is the Holy Sacrament with people grouped around it in a similar way. But instead of a series of walls and arches the sky is open, and on a cloud formation another group of figures appears, as in a vision: John and Mary resurrected, saints and angelic beings, all grouped around what we may call the Holy Trinity of Father, Son and – in the symbol of the dove – the Holy Spirit. What is closed, hidden, or veiled in the other picture is here open. Naturally people have also tried to name the different figures here, and they can indeed be identified. But in this picture Paul appears twice: once among the saints (far right) and, as far as I can determine, also as this special figure in front of the altar. Although Rudolf Steiner said nothing about Paul, he explained that this picture should never have been called the *Disputa,* because nothing is disputed. The altar and the sacrament are revealed by the appearance of the Trinity. We should try to imagine the pope looking at this picture, with the *School of Athens* behind him, and allow this image to stand before us as a preliminary to our further deliberations.

Let us try to understand the historic period in which these two pictures appeared. We know that they were painted in 1510 and 1511 during the rule of Pope Julius II, when Raphael was in Rome. There is no doubt that he painted them under the strong influence of two old men: of Julius II himself, who wanted to show something of his own ideas in these two pictures, and of Donato Bramante (1444–1514). At that time Bramante had planned St Peter's Basilica, seeing it as the centre of the world.

He influenced the young Raphael who was only 28 years of age in 1511. So we can imagine Raphael with these two old men behind him – Julius II and Bramante – who were very wise and powerful, but were also in many ways very evil.

If we look into the background of this period and see to which 33-year period they belong, we find it be a very special period beginning in 1485 and lasting until 1518. A large portion of Europe was under the control or influence of the Habsburgs; it was the beginning of the Renaissance, and the Reformation began in 1517. I will only mention a few events also from the 33-year periods leading up to this time – those beginning in 1452 and 1419 – and those following. In 1413 the period of the consciousness soul started. In the earlier period Joan of Arc (1412–31) was one of the leading figures. The Hundred Years' War between England and France took place. The Middle Ages were in decline, and something entirely new was starting to arise in human souls. This becomes apparent when in the next 33-year period a man like Nicholas of Cusa (1401–64) began to think in an entirely new way about human thinking. With Nicholas the rise of humanism all over Europe began. Then in 1483, two years before the following 33-year period started, Raphael was born.

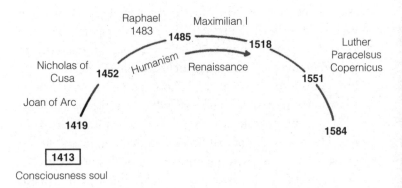

Let us leave this central 33-year period for a moment and move on to the next one, 1518 to 1551. I need only mention the names of Copernicus (1473–1543), Paracelsus (1493–1541) and Luther (1483–1546), or that the art of printing was now common, and we can understand that suddenly something entirely new occurred which is a tremendous step in the development of humanity. During that time Maximilian I was Holy Roman Emperor; Leonardo, Raphael and Michelangelo created their works of art in Italy, while in Germany Dürer, Veit Stoss, and many others appeared, so that what grew up was a complete revival of Greece: in a word, the Renaissance. This is the background of that special epoch, which was prepared at the beginning of the age of the consciousness soul with the first appearance of humanism in that leading spirit of Nicholas of Cusa, who was reborn to continue his work as Copernicus.[2] From this moment on the earth was no longer seen as the centre, and people began to discover the world through their sense-impressions and perceptions. The Renaissance then declined; the printed word and dead thought prepared what was to come later as modern science and technology.

Raphael lived at the peak of this important historic period, his birth preceded it by two years, and he died in 1520, two years after it had finished. He revealed something that had no precursor at all, and it is futile to ask who Raphael's master was. As a painter he had neither forerunner nor successor; he was self-contained and unique. In a lecture on Raphael's task, Rudolf Steiner said the following:

> One could say that in a certain sense the gods of Homer, which he described so magnificently almost a thousand years before the founding of Christianity, would lose something as we look back into antiquity, if we could not see how they have resurrected in the soul of Raphael, and in a certain sense have found completion through the mighty pictorial expression of Raphael's creations.[3]

Here Rudolf Steiner described Raphael as one in whose soul the heritage of Greece was fully alive. The wonder, the beauty, the complete fulfilment of human and earthly harmony, was all reborn in Raphael. It was during those few years that the Renaissance arose more or less around Raphael in Rome and Italy, and to a certain extent in other southern parts of Europe. We can see this as a kind of glory, how the world of Greece reappeared in Raphael like a historic memory. But in its colour, line and form it now appears in an essentially Christian manner, and we see something of this wonder and beauty of Greece in the picture of the *School of Athens.*

Now I would like to draw your attention to Rudolf Steiner's words about the two figures who appear in the centre of the picture (Plate 3). Here the name 'Timeo' is written, and there 'Etica'. However, Rudolf Steiner makes it quite clear that this is a later falsification in order that these figures be thought of as Aristotle and Plato, which is not only a mistake but in my opinion a deliberate distortion. The old man wearing a red cloak is pointing upwards; the younger, in blue, points forwards. The young figure looks at the older, who does not look into the distance, he just points, lost in deep inner contemplation.

When opening the new branch room in Cologne in 1912, Rudolf Steiner says the following.

> There is a picture in the Vatican, the *School of Athens* by
> Raphael. Even if this picture will one day have vanished,
> its reputation will live on. It will live on further because
> the creator of this picture, Raphael, felt the spirit of
> the Christian Word in a different way from popes and
> cardinals. Before our eyes stands the picture representing
> the story from the Acts of the Apostles, where the
> Athenians are gathered with all the men from olden
> times. Paul then steps among them and saying, 'You have
> long been speaking about the unknown god, have long
> been worshipping images of gods in your temples and

statues. But I want to speak about the spirit which works and lives in all existence. Nothing external can bring it to expression, but it lives and works in everything, and is also alive in us.' Many did not understand him, and turned away. Only a few understood him.

This scene stood before Raphael's eyes. He painted it onto the wall, and poured the spirit into one figure, even into the movement of his hand. This figure is not Aristotle. No, it is the one whom Raphael beheld in the spirit: Paul, speaking to the people about the Christ. There stands Paul, not Aristotle.[4]

Rudolf Steiner says this at a special moment, and he points out quite clearly and definitely that Raphael beheld in spirit the figure of Paul; Paul as described in that significant Chapter 17 of the Acts of the Apostles, when he entered Athens and spoke about the unknown God. Of course it is difficult to answer why Raphael's inner impulse was falsified, and why those who instructed him to paint these pictures, Julius II and Bramante, and later their followers, should try to wipe out Raphael's true intentions so completely. Rudolf Steiner refers to this picture in several other lectures, and allowed me to read some passages from them because I have the impression they are of great importance if we want to understand why Plato and Aristotle were superimposed on Paul and Dionysius, and why Rudolf Steiner made such a point of clarifying this mistake, or rather this falsification. In a lecture given five and a half years later, he said:

Often (but only later) called School of Athens, this fresco has had all kinds of things painted over it in course of time, as is the case with the word 'Etica,' which has been painted on the book held by a man standing at the centre, and 'Timeo' on another book – all of that painted in at a later date. The work has been spoiled in many ways, and we do not, of course, get the right idea in Rome of what it was like originally.

No one called it the *School of Athens* in Raphael's day; this is something that came later, but people then developed theories about it. We have to say that in the other painting *(Disputa)*, the world is represented truly as it is when we look out into infinite space and think of nature, not only as it presents itself to the senses, but full of everything that exists in eternity and temporality, and full also of those who have gone through the gates of death.[5]

Then Rudolf Steiner again referred to the mistake, saying that to understand the *School of Athens* we have also to see the *Disputa*. In another lecture he describes the two figures in the following way:

The middle figures are therefore to be understood like so: in one figure we see a man who is still younger, who has less life experience and thus talks more than someone who looks around at the surface of the Earth in order to learn from it where things come from; and in the other figure we see the gray old man who has done a lot of work on himself and already knows how to relate what he sees on Earth to the heavenly realm; and both of them are depicted alongside figures who are attempting to discover the causes of things, some of them through meditation, some through arithmetic, geometry and the like, some through interpretation of Scripture (so, through the written word), and some through the application of human reasoning.[6]

Now in this lecture Rudolf Steiner basically said, I don't mind whether you call these two Paul and Dionysius; what we should understand is that the one is a younger man, who lives more in the outer world, and the other is the older one, who is given to contemplation – and that these two central figures express something that was hidden until then: how human beings can approach higher worlds either by going outwards, or by inner contemplation.

The question stands before us: if the figure of Paul appeared to Raphael, why was his true intention falsified in the following centuries? It becomes more and more clear that Raphael was deeply occupied with Paul. Raphael tried in many different ways to grapple with the figure of Paul. Probably the greatest expert on Raphael in the history of art of our time – Oskar Fischel, who wrote a two volumes on Raphael (it was his life's work) – actually devoted a whole chapter to Raphael and St Paul. Also Hermann Grimm, the greatest of Raphael's biographers, wrote two chapters on Raphael and Paul. Fischel wrote of Raphael as a poet, 'Reverence for such a poet imposes a closer scrutiny into one of his favourite creations, the figure of St Paul.'[7]

Then he refers to the *Disputa*. I pointed out earlier that Paul appears twice – among the saints around the Holy Trinity, and down on earth in front of the holy sacrament. He then mentions that a sketch by Raphael of Paul was found (Plate 6), which is now in Oxford.* On this sketch Raphael wrote a poem in which he referred to an experience he had when being so intimately drawn to Paul. He describes his experience that he 'cannot bear witness to the enrapturing wonders' that he has seen, and to the 'ineffable words that may not be spoken.'[8]

Rudolf Steiner too refers to the deep connection of Paul and Raphael. It was during the last years of Raphael's life that picture after picture was painted and drawn of the Acts of the Apostles and of Paul, for instance of the conversion of Paul (Plate 9). There are other depictions of Paul, two of which I would like to show, so that we may have an impression of how Raphael occupied himself so intimately with the figure of Paul.

There is one of St Cecilia. The figure next to Cecilia is Paul, and we can clearly see the similarity to the younger figure in the *School of Athens*. In the picture of St Cecilia Paul is contemplative, meditating. Then there is the picture of Paul preaching in Athens on the Areopagus (Plate 5). It is clearly the same individuality,

---

* The sketch was in the Bodleian Library in Oxford when König gave these lectures, but today it is in the Ashmolean Museum, Oxford.

and looking at the head of each figure, we can gain an impression of Raphael's vision of Paul.

In 1510, the *School of Athens* and the *Disputa* were painted in the Vatican. But in the same year something of the greatest importance happened in Rome. In a special way Rudolf Steiner described how in 1510,

> a man from Northern Europe went up the Penitents' Steps in Rome on his knees; it was said that anyone who climbed those steps pleased God so much that he would be relieved of one day in purgatory for each step ... And while that man climbed those steps, he had a vision, a vision that showed him the pointlessness of religious acts like climbing steps on his knees in order to save himself from days in purgatory – a vision that made him break all relations with the world that Raphael ... was painting ... that man from the North was Luther.[9]

Martin Luther, like Raphael, was born in 1483. Raphael on March 28 – on Good Friday – and Rudolf Steiner called him a 'spring birth' *(eine Frühlingsgeburt),* using this word with a special intention. Luther was born on November 10 of that same year – an 'autumn birth', one could say. Steiner described how Luther, after having had this vision, returned to Germany determined to eradicate what he had met in Rome; determined to bring about a reformation that would utterly destroy the Renaissance, with its joy and solace derived from its beauty and wonder. And if we think of those reformers who came after him – Calvin and others – we can gradually imagine the darkness and poverty that tried to enter the world – strengthening the emptiness, poverty and death forces of the consciousness soul.

Referring to something we have learned from Rudolf Steiner we can imagine how in Europe in the ninth century the spirituality of the east was suppressed and destroyed under Pope Nicholas in Rome. No spirituality was to enter Europe. The Eastern Orthodox Church, still filled with holy wisdom, separated from the Roman Church. This was in the ninth century. In the sixteenth century, a new element started: the rebirth of Greece in the light of Pauline Christianity. And this rebirth of Greece in the light of Pauline Christianity was expressed in the two pictures, the *School of Athens* and the *Disputa*. But against this came the influence of Luther, Zwingli and others from the north. The reformation from the south that wanted to renew Christianity was completely wiped out from the north.

At the same time the geographical discoveries started – America was found – and development and primacy of the western world started. Raphael's intentions – the reformation from the south, a Pauline reformation of Christianity in the garment of Greece – were completely wiped out. A hundred years later something else started to come from the south. What had been prevented was replaced in an entirely different disguise. Jesuitism replaced what the Pauline reformation did not achieve. Of course Luther spoke about the Epistles of Paul, and the reformers tried to bring about a certain kind of Pauline Christianity, but what Raphael had tried enkindle did not come about. And in order to wipe out the knowledge of this reformation completely, Paul and Dionysius the Areopagite were replaced by Aristotle and Plato. Now we can understand why this was done, and see the reason why Rudolf Steiner time and again tried to make this historic fact as clear as possible.

What is really shown in the *School of Athens?* Earlier I pointed to the complete harmony and symmetry of the right and left side. Raphael painted in such a way that the alert observer looks into a mirror as it were. The three arches above the pillars, spanning everything, are mirrored and the observer appears to look into his own skull. There the thoughts of the seven liberal arts show themselves in the form of human figures, and into this scene the two men enter – the two central figures – with an entirely new power and new force, sweeping away what lived in the School of Athens, bringing an entirely new impulse into it. The older figure, Dionysius the Areopagite, points upwards, while

31

Paul points forwards. What is he pointing at? He is pointing to the picture opposite, to the *Disputa,* instructing his companion, who was one of the last pupils of the mystery school of Eleusis, 'Transform your mystery knowledge, look at the image of the Holy Trinity.'

At that moment the first esoteric Christian school started. From that time on it continued through centuries right into the ninth century until spirituality was suppressed by Rome. But during this ninth century the School of Dionysius gradually transformed into the mysteries of the Holy Grail. And this was what Raphael divined when time and again he tried to imbue himself with the experiences of Paul. He wrestled with understanding the being of Paul. He tried, under the auspices of papal Rome, to bring about the reformation from the south. Raphael was not only this youthful, beautiful, reappearance of the ideals of Greece: he was permeated with Pauline Christianity. He was one who tried to blaze a trail because he was the reincarnation of John the Baptist. He did not succeed. He took it up again when he was born as Novalis, and what Novalis could not fulfil arose again through Rudolf Steiner in science of the spirit. That is why it is so important that we learn to understand these two pictures. They bear witness to something which began in the sixteenth century and only now arises again in history: a stream in which we ourselves can serve.

Plate 1. Raphael, *The School of Athens*

Plate 2. Raphael, *The Disputa*

Plate 3. Raphael, detail from the *School of Athens*

Plate 4. Raphael, detail from the *Disputa*

Plate 5. Raphael, *Paul Preaching in Athens*
(© Victoria and Albert Museum, London)

Plate 6. Raphael, *Sketch for the Disputa* (Ashmolean, Oxford)

Plate 7. Raphael, *St Cecilia*

Plate 8. Raphael, *Paul before the Proconsul and the Blinding of Elymas* (Acts 13:8–11)

Plate 9. Peter van Aelst, *The Conversion of Paul*, tapestry after Raphael (Getty Images/DeAgostini)

Plate 10. Michelangelo, *Pietà*

2

The Mithras Mysteries, Eleusis and the Rosicrucians

Lecture 2,
Sunday, February 25, 1962

In the last lecture we tried to approach Raphael's great picture known as the *School of Athens,* And we came to understand that it is not, as usually described, the School of Athens at the time of the two great philosophers, Plato and Aristotle, but that it was a different moment Raphael wanted to put before the world. It was the meeting of deep significance when Paul, the apostle, entered the city of Athens and encountered Dionysius the Areopagite. These two men, meeting among all the great philosophers, stood quite apart from them, were listened to by only a few. In them the end of the old mystery knowledge met with the beginning of the new mysteries of Christianity. This is what one could say about this picture. In it the past meets the future: the pre-Christian age clasps hands with the Christianity to come.

Now, all this sounds quite plausible, quite understandable and quite interesting; but it is much more. Paul, at that time a more or less unknown man, came to Athens and met one who no doubt was an initiate, because only an initiate would have recognised what Paul had to say. Not only that, but he became a pupil of Paul, and with and through him founded a new mystery school from which many things emanated. I will go into some detail about the individuality of Dionysius, so that a living picture of him may start to arise before us. Some writings of Dionysius have come down to us. One is called *Celestial Hierarchy,* which is about the angels, another is called *About Divine Names.* However, it has become clear through scientific investigation that these writings are not by the same Dionysius who met and became a pupil of Paul, but were written in about the sixth century. The author of these writings is therefore called Pseudo-Dionysius, who is seen as a kind of swindler who took on the name of Dionysius the Areopagite who is named in the Acts of the Apostles. According to syntax and many other things these writings can only be from the sixth century, and they are regarded as falsely attributed.

Rudolf Steiner also draws our attention to this fact, but then tells us (on several occasions) that in former times esoteric knowledge was never written down; it was only handed on from individual to individual, from master to pupil by word of mouth. No-one ever dared to put real esoteric knowledge in writing. Steiner also explains that the master of the school which was founded by the Apostle Paul during the first century in Athens always carried the name of Dionysius the Areopagite. It was not the name of an individual but the name of a holy office. The one who officiated as a master in this school had the name Dionysius. And the Dionysius who wrote the books which have come down to us, which we can read in the original or in translation, lived in the sixth century, but he was a true Dionysius the Areopagite. He carried similar wisdom, similar esoteric knowledge, to that of the Dionysius who met Paul. In the sixth century – the time of the decline of the fourth post-Atlantean period – the power of thought came to dominance, tradition in esotericism was laid aside, and esoteric knowledge was written down and entered the stream of outer history.

If we try to understand what happened in the course of the sixth century, we find that nothing is known about this late Dionysius the Areopagite. There are certain theories, but I don't think any one is of value. We do not know him at all. But we can sense what he must have felt and experienced when he found it necessary to write his knowledge on parchment. He was the last one with this knowledge; the mystery school had to be dissolved. What was written down had been living wisdom filling human souls and spirits, and was now dying or dead knowledge, handed over to the stream of history. Like a boat without oars and rudder, it drifted away. And now it is interesting to find the different shores of the stream where from time to time this boat landed – one could almost say 'stranded'. There was an individual like John Scotus Erigena, who suddenly came across the writings and took them up. The great Thomas Aquinas and Albertus Magnus, tried to understand these writings and tried to assimilate them into the teachings of the Church. Here and there, even well into the Renaissance, this wisdom began to fertilise human minds.

We can ask ourselves, what kind of wisdom was it? We have seen that two people met, one representing the old, the other representing the new mysteries; that an esoteric school arose out of this meeting; and that this esoteric school lasted for about six centuries; that it left its protected abode and was cast into the unknown stream of events. Where did the wisdom come from which Raphael shows in this picture?

There is something that can only be called the *Urweltweisheit* – we may translate it as the 'primeval wisdom'. If we have the courage to understand what this primeval wisdom, this *Urweltweisheit,* is, we would have to imagine this primeval wisdom consisting of the thoughts of divine beings before they created the human being on earth. The primeval wisdom is the totality, the universal sum of primeval ideas according to which human beings, the earth and our planetary system gradually came into being. The primeval wisdom is the wisdom which has its origin before Old Saturn came into being. On Saturn 'bodies' were created, mirroring divine beings, and into these bodies divine beings poured their own existence. This was then dissolved. Then the Old Sun came into existence and again disappeared. The Old Moon came into being. And at last the Earth. Out of Saturn, Sun, Moon and Earth the spheres of the cosmos were increasingly created, as well as the kingdoms of nature and man. Step by step the individuality expressed itself in a human being. All this and much more is meant by primeval wisdom.

This primeval wisdom gradually was reflected downwards, so the growing human mind was able to catch one or another of the lightbeams of that primeval wisdom. In the light of this wisdom human beings unfolded on earth: in the light of this wisdom human beings created the different civilisations.

Through the millennia, especially after the Atlantean continent disappeared, there were great migrations. First there was the journey from the west to the east in order to bring about the awakening of human intellect under the leadership of the great Manes. Then, going back from the east to the west, humankind gradually lost the immediate clairvoyant connection with the world of the spirit. Over time an ever-smaller group of people remained the carriers of this primeval wisdom, while the others, especially after the beginning of the Kali Yuga in the third millennium before Christ, became increasingly at home on the earth and in the world of maya. The seven holy Rishis (of whom Rudolf Steiner so often spoke) intoned singing words – one can only express it in this way. And through these singing words, which we would no longer understand, holy primeval wisdom was poured into the surroundings. Some heard it; a few understood it and carried it further. Through the mysteries of Persia, of Egypt, Babylonia, even through the mysteries of Greece, the primeval wisdom was carried further, even into Europe.

And then the Mystery of Golgotha took place. And with the Mystery of Golgotha this primeval wisdom underwent a tremendous rejuvenation and renewal. We may imagine that the rejuvenation of the primeval wisdom happened for the first time within a single individual in the experience which Paul had at Damascus – this experience of the living Christ in the ether form. We know that Paul, through his learning and former existence when he was known as Saul, was an initiate of the old mysteries – of the Greek mysteries as well as the Hebrew mysteries. In this moment that Paul became blind to outer light, the rejuvenation of the old mystery knowledge, of the old primeval wisdom, took place. With this rejuvenated knowledge he entered Athens and met Dionysius the Areopagite.

I would like to quote from two or three of Rudolf Steiner's lectures in which he spoke of this event, so that we may have the possibility to see it from various sides. In the introductory lecture of the cycle on the hierarchies in 1909, he said:

> When ancient wisdom was restored at the beginning of our era, human beings were again directed to the starry realms so that humanity might not completely lose its connection with primeval spiritual wisdom. They were told in clear, direct words that, when they looked up to the heavens with their physical eyes, they would find there not only a material universe, but also realms filled with spirit.
>
> The most intimate pupil of St Paul, Dionysius the Areopagite, clearly proclaimed in Athens that out in space there was not only matter, but that when the soul arose with inner awareness into the expanses of the universe, it would find spiritual beings who are above humanity in evolutionary development. Dionysius coined different terms from those used previously, for otherwise people would have thought that he referred only to material entities.[1]

Rudolf Steiner pointed in these few sentences to the rejuvenation of the primeval knowledge through the Mystery of Golgotha, and called Dionysius the most intimate pupil of the Apostle Paul. He continued:

Dionysius, the pupil of the St Paul, had in mind the same worlds the Rishis spoke of. Dionysius clearly wished to emphasise that he was referring to spiritual matters. So he deliberately chose words which he knew would be taken spiritually – that is, he spoke of Angels, Archangels, Archai, Powers, Mights, Dominions, Thrones, Cherubim, and Seraphim. But people had completely forgotten what they once knew. If the connection between the terminology of Dionysius the Areopagite and the Rishis had been understood, one would have known that the 'Moon' the Rishis referred to, and the 'angelic realm' in other mysteries, are one and the same thing. One might have heard the word *Mercury* on the one hand, and the word *Archangel* on the other, and would have known that they are one and the same. *Archai* and *Venus* refer to the same realm, as do *Sun* and *Powers*. On hearing the word *Mars,* one would have had the feeling of rising to the Mights [Dynameis]. The word *Dominions* in the school of Dionysius corresponds to Jupiter, and the term *Saturn* to the Thrones.

In wider circles, this knowledge had disappeared and was no longer known. As science became more and more materialistic, the old names, which had once denoted spiritual realities, remained. But now increasingly they applied only to matter. In contrast to this materialistic stream, there did exist a spiritual stream that referred to Archangels, Angels and so on. But this stream had lost the connection with the physical expression of these spiritual beings.

Here Rudolf Steiner points to the fact that this archetypal or primeval wisdom which the seven holy Rishis knew in the eighth millennium before Christ, which they received and poured out, united itself with the School of Athens, with the school of Dionysius the Areopagite. And therefore Dionysius could point out, as it were, 'What you call the moon, when you look at this celestial body that reflects the lights of the sun, you can also call Angel. If you look at Mercury, you can call it Archangel, if you look at Venus you can call it Archai, and if you look at the sun you may call it Exousiai. From the one side it is existence, from the other side it is matter.'

And then Rudolf Steiner adds, 'Thus we see how the primeval wisdom penetrated into the school founded by St Paul through Dionysius.' This is the first conclusion to which we can come: that in the school of Dionysius, which was founded through Paul, we meet divine wisdom. We meet something again which, before the beginning of all existence and then throughout the whole of evolution before the time of Christ, has been the *Urweltweisheit,* the primeval wisdom.

What was the character of this school? In this school, like in all mystery schools, truth was revealed to the pupils only after hard and earnest preparation. Then Rudolf Steiner pointed out something which is of very great importance, and characterises the way in which this school was conducted:

> Whilst Paul was preaching to the world at large, his
> disciples went through their esoteric experiences in
> Athens. The spirit of the school continued through long
> periods of time, and because of this the individual who
> bore this esoteric truth would always be given the same
> name. The School of Athens continued for centuries and
> the highest of the teachers was always called Dionysius.
> This is why the one who wrote the things down in
> the sixth century, when writing had become more of a
> custom, also bore that name.[2]

Some of these things I described earlier, but we should hold one image before us. Rudolf Steiner said that Paul was preaching to the world at large, in Rome, Corinth and wherever he went, while in the School of Athens esoteric knowledge was imparted. As far as we know, Paul never returned to Athens. He founded the school together with Dionysius – or we may say through Dionysius.

Paul continued on his missionary journeys to Asia Minor and to Europe. But the seed of this esoteric school remained. And it remained in such a way that a centre of Christian esotericism was created, which lasted for several centuries.

It is not easy to describe what was taught in this school. Only through some indications of Rudolf Steiner's can we start to divine – one can only describe it as such – in which way the pupils were led. The school was led in a twofold way. On the one hand (and this you can read in the books of Dionysius) it is important to go out into the world, to study, to name and to understand: and how one should always go one step further, from thing to thing, from being to being, from event to event to gather knowledge. On the other hand, he teaches that there is nothing whatsoever that can be compared to divine existence: whatever you meet, whatever you study, whatever you learn, will not help you at all to reach any kind of esoteric knowledge. Only if you give up your knowledge, will you be able to arrive at something which can help you to grasp the Godhead.

> You speak about beings, [Dionysius said] you can also speak about divine beings. You can try to imagine them. But only if you come so far that you learn to understand something which is higher than existence, beyond existence, only then will you learn to grasp something of divine existence. The same is true of nature: you study the plants, you study the minerals, you study the animals, you study man. All this is existence or 'being'. But only if you learn to train your thoughts in such a form will you understand that the Godhead stands beyond such existence or 'being'.[3]

Rudolf Steiner described Dionysius thus:

> Now, in his mind, Dionysius confronted the mighty Mystery of Golgotha. He dwelled in the intellectual culture of his time. Anybody studying the writings of

Dionysius sees – regardless of who Dionysius was – how immersed this man was in all that the intellectual culture of his time had produced. He was a well educated Greek but at the same time a man whose whole personality was imbued with the magnitude of the Mystery of Golgotha.[4]

We can ask ourselves, where does Dionysius come from? Can we say something more about him than that he was a highly educated man of his time, a true Greek but knowing the truth of the newly-arisen Christianity? We also know through Rudolf Steiner that Dionysius was a pupil, an initiate, of the mysteries of Eleusis – and he was probably given the name of Dionysius there, for at the centre of the mysteries of Eleusis stood the god Dionysius, at least of the outer mysteries. In Schuré's great drama of Eleusis the central figure is the god Dionysius. Rudolf Steiner related that the Eleusinian mysteries were a continuation of the mysteries of Mithras which started in the third post-Atlantean Epoch. I think we can imagine that the land of Sumer or Mesopotamia was the home of the mysteries of Mithras.

The Mithraic mysteries permeated the whole civilisation of Rome and also the ritual of the Roman Catholic Church. The Holy Mass is nothing but a metamorphosis of the Mithraic mysteries. They were probably founded four or five thousand years before Christ, in the land of Sumer. And these Mithraic mysteries were conducted in such a way that they tried to lead the human spirit to the inner experience of the body – to the experience of the mysteries of the physical, etheric and astral body – to lead man on the mystic path to an insight into the glory and wonder of the creative powers of the innermost human existence. They concentrated human beings into their earthly and cosmic form and gestalt.

Out of these Mithraic mysteries gradually, from the seventh century BC onwards, the Eleusinian mysteries developed. In the Eleusinian mysteries people were taught in a different way. They were not hemmed into the body. They were taught to meet the creative powers, to encounter what we called the primeval wisdom, the ideas of creative existence, not within but outside themselves. Human souls were led outside into the heights and widths of the whole of the planetary cosmos. And there they had to learn that whatever they found in the sphere of the sun, of Saturn and the moon, of Jupiter and Mars, and whichever divine beings they met there could only explain how nature was created on the earth, but could never explain the nature of man. 'O Man, know yourself. But know that through all knowledge your own existence is not revealed.'

In the Eleusinian mysteries the pupil, in preparation for initiation, was shown a piece of lead, the metal lead, and was told, 'Look upon this; it is the corpse of what was once alive. It was created at a time when you were still in the surroundings of this earthly sphere. It was created by powers, by beings, which you can no longer behold, but which live and surround the planet Saturn. From there these Saturnine beings poured their strength and existence into the earth. And what remained from this act of creation you can see here in this metal, in this lead; but you must know that the powers which created lead once upon a time streamed into yourself. These are the same powers which make it possible for you to remember. Your memory is nothing but the other side of this metal lead – the other expression of what streamed from Saturn into the foundations of earth existence.'

And in similar ways the master, the initiate, spoke about the moon and silver, about Venus and copper, Mars and iron, Jupiter and tin. He explained how the form of our existence comes from the sun; how the powers of metabolism originate from the moon. How all these metals, our inner being and outer planetary existence, how all this is one.

After this preparation the pupils were led into the inner chamber of the temple, and there they were placed before a huge figure. This figure they learned to see and to understand as the figure of the Father of all Creation. This figure of the Father of all Creation had in one hand the various powers of the metals – of lead and tin, of iron and gold, of silver and copper and mercury. Then the pupil began in inner images, in true imaginations, to see how the Father handed over these metals to another figure who stood next to the great one; this was the figure of the Mother. From below the Mother took the gift of the metals from the Father and surrounded it with calcium and silica, with all the various substances of the earth. And the pupil started to understand how the body of the Earth was created.

When this first step of initiation was completed, and after further preparation, the pupil was led into another cell, and was shown a different figure. This figure was the Mother who had a child on her lap. And the pupil was told, 'This is Jakos, the new god who will come.' From the sixth or fifth century BC onwards the pupil in the Eleusinian Mysteries was prepared with these words to recognise and receive what in the streets of Athens was called 'the unknown god' – the child Jakos. Dionysius, as a pupil of the Eleusinian mysteries, had experienced this and brought the knowledge of the child Jakos with him.

Now we can understand the meeting of the knowledge, the esoteric wisdom in Dionysus, and the reality, the experience of the Christ in Paul. We can only really understand the mission of Paul by realising that – never having known the Christ, and having persecuted Jesus – in the experience of Damascus he recognised the being who permeated the crucified Jesus. This recognition in Paul's direct experience was united with the mystery wisdom of the child of the living godhead. And this union, this communion, between Jakos of the Eleusinian mysteries and the being of Christ as beheld by Paul at Damascus, is the foundation of the esoteric School of Athens.

This school laid the seed for all esoteric Christianity in the ensuing centuries. In 1907 Rudolf Steiner elaborated on this theme, speaking about the two ways which human beings of today can take to gain esoteric knowledge – the Christian way and the Rosicrucian way:

The newest way of attaining wisdom is the Rosicrucian
path. This path does not point us to the past but to
the future, to those conditions which we will still live
through. Through precise methods the pupil is taught
to develop in himself the wisdom that exists as a seed in
every human being.

It is the modern way of Rosicrucianism, the esoteric path
appropriate for our time, that seeks to unfold the mystery
knowledge which is latent in every human being. Steiner
continues:

This path had been partially prepared long before the
time of Christianity. It took on a special form through
that great initiate, Dionysius the Areopagite, who in the
esoteric school of Paul at Athens inaugurated the training
from which all later esoteric wisdom and training have
been derived.[5]

This inner training was prepared in the pre-Christian centuries
and through the meeting of Paul and Dionysius took on its
special form in the School of Athens, which laid the seed of all
esoteric Christianity in the following centuries.

Returning to our theme of the relation between Paul and the
Holy Grail, we looked first for the seed from where we could
start. Now we can go back to Raphael's picture of the *School of
Athens* and ask, what did Raphael actually try to show humanity?
In this picture, in the Madonnas which he painted and in all
other forms of his art, Raphael tried to unveil the esoteric
teaching of the School of Athens, to remind his contemporaries
that esoteric Christianity existed. In the Vatican he achieved
this. But we have to remember that Raphael's true opponent
at that time was none other than Martin Luther. From the
north came the Reformation: and against the Reformation the
tremendous power of Jesuitism arose. Between the Reformation
and Jesuitism esoteric Christianity was crushed. Only in the
School of Athens can we still see Raphael's innermost intentions.

Read Rudolf Steiner's Last Address. On the last occasion he could still stand and speak, he described the path which the spirit of Raphael took through the planetary spheres, as if he wanted show how the new Eleusinian mysteries revealed themselves in Raphael and in Novalis.

I hope that this approach is a help for us to understand the significance of gathering together the first building blocks of a Pauline Christianity. It is perhaps significant that just at a time when people try to reach the planetary spheres and penetrate into these realms not by spiritual but by material means with all the achievements of modern science, we are challenged to know the other side, the spiritual side.* We are called on to know that the moon is connected with the Angels, Mercury with the Archangels, Venus with the Archai and the sun with the Exousiai, so that we may work for the true evolution of the human being and humanity.

---

* The months before this lecture was given saw the launch of the first manned space flights by the Soviet Union and then by the United States.

3

The Sixth Century

Lecture 3,
Sunday, April 1, 1962

How is Paul connected with the Holy Grail? This is not an easy question, and it is by no means obvious how this question can be approached. There are signs here or there indicating that Paul and all his teaching might be connected with the Holy Grail, but it would be unjustified to assume that it is so. And we should not simply go forward on this assumption regardless of historical facts and regardless of spiritual insight. Let us approach this question as an enigma, and let us search for an answer, for which there is no ready-made solution. It is as if lifting a veil behind which we might find a sign about Paul and the Holy Grail.

We started by looking at the picture painted by Raphael called the *School of Athens,* and in this picture, with the help of Rudolf Steiner, we gradually saw this very special moment, this great historic moment, when Paul entered the city of Athens and met Dionysius the Areopagite. Dionysius became his pupil, and Paul founded the esoteric school with him. But Paul himself was the founder, and this again we know through Rudolf Steiner.

We tried to imagine who this Dionysius was, and we learned that he was an initiate of the Eleusinian mysteries. As an initiate he was the first to unite the newly understood Christianity with the tradition of the mysteries as they were taught in Eleusis. Here the new Christian revelation met with the wisdom of the old mysteries. What was still alive and imparted in such mysteries as those of Eleusis was the last remnant of the archetypal wisdom, the *Urweltweisheit,* that was once alive. This primeval wisdom gradually came down from heaven to earth, from the east to the west, from the Rishis, through Zarathustra, through all the other hundreds and thousands of initiates through human history before Christ. This primeval wisdom was streaming down through all these human souls permeating more and more human beings who became pupils and became initiates of the old mysteries. Finally this primordial wisdom entered the esoteric school of Athens on the one hand through Paul and on the other through Dionysius the Areopagite. I would like to quote again these important words of Rudolf Steiner:

> When ancient wisdom was restored at the beginning of our era, human beings were again directed to the starry realms so that humanity might not completely lose its connection with primeval spiritual wisdom. They were told in clear, direct words that, when they looked up to the heavens with their physical eyes, they would find there not only a material universe, but also realms filled with spirit.
>
> The most intimate pupil of St Paul, Dionysius the Areopagite, clearly proclaimed in Athens that out in space there was not only matter, but that when the soul arose with inner awareness into the expanses of the universe, it would find spiritual beings who are above humanity in evolutionary development. Dionysius coined different terms from those used previously, for otherwise people would have thought that he referred only to material entities. When the Rishis spoke of spiritual hierarchies, their words expressed what Greek and Roman wisdom expressed in their ascending universe of Moon, Mercury,

Mars, Venus, Jupiter and Saturn. Dionysius, the pupil
of the St Paul, had in mind the same worlds the Rishis
spoke of. Dionysius clearly wished to emphasise that he
was referring to spiritual matters. So he deliberately chose
words which he knew would be taken spiritually – that is,
he spoke of Angels, Archangels, Archai, Powers, Mights,
Dominions, Thrones, Cherubim, and Seraphim.[1]

The stronger we learn to understand what Rudolf Steiner
called *Urweltweisheit,* the primeval wisdom, the more vividly and
clear will be our concept of what this School of Athens was in
truth. This is important because, as we heard last time in another
quotation, Rudolf Steiner said that whatever developed as
Christian esotericism came out of this school that Paul founded.

We can ask ourselves if there is any indication in the Letters
of Paul in which he refers to himself as the founder of such an
esoteric school in Athens, besides the description of his experience
before Damascus. There is an indication, which to my mind is of
the greatest importance, in the Second Letter to the Corinthians:

Since we are speaking of things about which one may
praise oneself – actually I do not expect much to be
gained by that – then I must also speak of the visions
and revelations in which the Lord has shown himself
to me. I know a man, living in Christ; fourteen years
ago – whether in the body or in a condition freed of the
body, I do not know; God knows it – he was transported
into the third heavenly sphere, and about this same man
I know – whether he was in the body, or in a condition
freed of the body, I do not know, God knows it – he was
transported into Paradise and perceived unspoken words
which may never be spoken by human mouth. On behalf
of this man I will praise myself. If I look to my earthly,
personal nature, I can only praise my weakness.

It would by no means be foolish of me if I wanted to
praise myself. I speak the truth. But I refrain from it, so

> that no one should have a better opinion of me than he
> can form for himself by what he sees and hears of me.
> That also applies to the wealth of revelations which I
> have been granted. (Cor.12:1–6)[2]

Here Paul speaks of a man who was lifted up into the third
heaven, meaning that his spirit reached right up to the first
hierarchy, experiencing what he calls 'unspoken words which
may never be spoken by human mouth.' He was initiated into
the highest regions of the spiritual world. But who was Paul
speaking of when he said 'I know a man'? He did not say that he
knew himself. But there is a strange ambiguity in Paul's words,
that allow us to sense that Paul is really speaking of himself here.
After this experience he is a twofold being: a man whom he
knows, and also himself, the one whom his followers can meet
in the body. He clearly distinguishes between his soul-and-spirit
being and his ordinary existence.

This clearly indicates that Paul was not only an initiate in the
old mysteries, in the Jewish mysteries and Pharisaic teachings,
but that the Christ himself had initiated him. I think that we
would not be wrong in assuming that during the three days
following the revelation at Damascus, when Paul was blind and
did not take food or drink, he was lifted up into the region of the
third heaven, that he encountered Paradise, that he was initiated
and returned as an initiate, and was then a twofold being.

Now we may understand a bit more why Rudolf Steiner said
that the true follower of John the Evangelist was the Apostle
Paul. Lazarus was initiated, raised by the Christ in the same way
as was Paul. These two initiations took place in entirely different
ways, but they are the first two initiations which took place
directly through Christ.

If we look at the teachings of Dionysius the Areopagite, we
meet something that has puzzled modern theologians a great
deal. In Dionysius' various writings one could almost say that two
completely different theologies are given, begging the question,
how is it possible that one writer can say one thing and then the

opposite, both with the same strength and impact? This would not be so astonishing today, but for Dionysius it is of course very unusual because he gives the impression that he believes what he says, and yet he says two opposite things. One of the writings is called *The Divine Names,* another is called *The Celestial Hierarchy,* and (connected to the hierarchies) *The Ecclesiastical Hierarchy,* about the body of the Church. In these writings you will find roughly the following. I say 'roughly' because it is exceedingly difficult to understand the ancient text through the modern translations.

On the one hand Dionysius wrote that the soul searches for the divine world, and in so doing it is necessary to understand and to observe in all the things of nature the good, the beautiful, the perfection that is contained in all that which is around us – be it a flower or mineral, or man or beast, or the heaven, stars or the wind. In all that there is, in each living and non-living thing, we should try to find and unlock its meaning. In other words we should try increasingly to see through the outer side, and, like Goethe, find the archetype in its fullness behind the outer side. And the more we do this – so Dionysius tells us – the more we will be able to give these things their proper names: and in doing so we will gradually approach the Godhead, though never reach it. For when we name something (and I am speaking in a neo-Platonic sense) we utter emanations from the Godhead; you could also say that we re-create the creations of the Godhead. Dionysius says if we penetrate beyond the material existence of a flower, experiencing form and colour we will find the meaning behind the form and colour; and the meaning will reveal the name to us. And in finding the name we meet the creator-being of that flower. But this creator-being of the flower is again an emanation of the Godhead. And so we will find hundreds, thousands, innumerable emanations from the Godhead, but we will never reach the Godhead.

The opposite, or second, way Dionysius wrote, was that whatever you name, will hide God from you. Whatever you call by its name will hinder you from meeting the Godhead. Do not even try to do this as you will be led astray. Instead of walking directly to meet God, you will go into many different directions without ever finding the true road.

These are the two opposite statements of Dionysius the Areopagite. One is the path towards the names, the other leads directly to the Godhead. Rudolf Steiner showed both to be true, for neither one nor the other path can be taken independently. Only at the crossing-point of these two paths can the Godhead be found. Steiner said:

> If a man takes either path alone he will never find the
> divine, but if he takes both paths, then he will find the way
> to the divine from that point at which the two paths meet.[3]

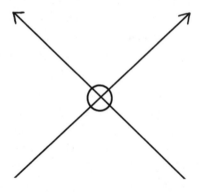

Let us return to this very special experience to which Paul refers in the Second Letter to the Corinthians, where he speaks of himself as a twofold being, the one who was lifted up and the other one who is in his body. This point to nothing but this twofold way. What does this mean? The Godhead reveals itself there where the 'I am' of man and the wisdom of the world meet. We can name the world from the lowest to the highest existence. We can name the Angels and Archangels, as we name plants and animals, as we name our fellow human beings and those who have lived and those who are going to live, as we name the stars and the trees, the stones and the seas, the rivers and lakes. We can name everything. But as soon as we are self-aware beings, we cannot name ourselves. The 'I am' – at least the 'I am' itself – is nameless. The 'I am', as soon as it is named, withdraws into its own existence. The 'I am' is to us – though we are it – nameless. But if the 'I am' and the names of the worlds meet – if my 'I am' goes through all the regions of existence up to the regions of higher existence – then I am both here in the everyday world and there in higher existence, I am nameless: but the world is named. In some ways this is like the last possible essence of what was once primeval wisdom. In this light we can see that for Paul and Saul both names were justified. They were not before and after; he was Saul until his death and yet he was Paul. Because within life he had died already and had risen from Saul to Paul. This was not difficult for people at that time to understand.

The connection of these two ways – the understanding of these two ways – was something quite obvious to the leading personalities of that age. They still knew that only by 'I' and 'non-I' – by the meeting of the world and the 'I am' – can the Godhead be reached. This wisdom continued throughout the first Christian centuries, increasingly watered down, up to the time of the thirteenth century when Thomas Aquinas and Albertus Magnus drank from the last drops of this water of wisdom. Then it came to a complete end. Rudolf Steiner described this in the lecture I just quoted.

But the understanding of what Dionysius the Areopagite taught had already begun to end earlier. In the fourth century after Christ a curtain came down when Christianity became the state religion of the Roman Empire, when Constantinople was founded by Constantine, that Arianism was declared heretical.*

---

* Arianism is a Christian theological doctrine concerning the relationship of the Son to the Father God, named after Arius *(c.* 250–336). It was declared heretical at the First Council of Nicaea in 325.

All this had to come about. Around the same time, in the year 333, human thinking became pale, a condition from which it has suffered ever since. How did the School of Athens survive? How was the tradition and teaching of this school handed down? We have no historic records, because the wisdom of Dionysius was not written down until the year 533 (Rudolf Steiner gave this date in one of his lectures).

There are certain descriptions which Rudolf Steiner gave about the first three centuries of Christianity. He said that people had quite a different ability to think and to imagine during these first three centuries. It was really a curtain which came down at the time of Constantine. Before that the mystery schools in the east were still open and pupils were initiated. Certain possibilities were there to reach into the spirit-world. And in these mystery schools the Mithraic mysteries continued all over Europe, especially along the Danube, as well as into what today is France, Spain and Italy. Especially the Roman legionaries followed these Mithraic mysteries. Thus, alongside Christian ritual, the rituals of Mithras continued. This was the one aspect.

The other aspect was the last remnants of wisdom. It is exceedingly interesting that Rudolf Steiner described this last remnant of wisdom as an 'etheric astronomy'. During the first three centuries for those who were endowed with this wisdom it was quite clear and obvious that human beings entered this earth from a sphere that lay far behind the planetary spheres, and which later on was called the 'crystal heaven'. Human beings came out of this crystal heaven, step by step passing through the spheres of the planets to enter the earthly abode.

And on entering the earth they not only brought the form of their body, the forms of the organs; they also brought with them, inscribed into all these forms, the outlines of their destiny. Destiny and constitution – these are the words Rudolf Steiner uses – were one and the same. They were the remnant of what human beings had gone through when coming down to earth. And here on earth they still lived under the guidance of the planets, under the guidance of the powers of the crystal heaven.

But then gradually these two streams met: the stream of the ritual of the mysteries and the stream of wisdom. We need to understand that this image of Mithras kneeling on the bull and killing it. The initiates understood the meaning of this image. They knew that if a human being, having descended through the planetary spheres, entered earth existence without anything else happening, he would never become a human being, but would appear like a bull. In the bull all the planetary spheres, all the powers of the crystal heaven, all the elements are in complete equilibrium. But man is more. Man can only be a real human being if something new, something which only comes from the sun, rides on top of the bull. If this is understood, then the nature of the 'I am' of man can be approached.

I am describing this in such detail because I have the impression it is of the greatest importance that we learn to see it in connection with what we have spoken of just before. The teachings of Paul and the twofold way taught by Dionysius everywhere disappear. But during these first three centuries both esoteric and exoteric Christianity became increasingly known and widespread. Rudolf Steiner described it as follows:

> Now there exited schools of wisdom in the East up to
> the fourth century that by and by received reports and
> became aware of the Mystery of Golgotha, of Christ
> ... These schools then attempted to spread a certain
> teaching throughout the world, and for a time there was
> a tendency to let flow into the Mithras cult what agrees
> with the following supersensible perception: the true
> Mithras is the Christ; Mithras is his predecessor ... To
> turn the Mithra worship into a worship of Christ was
> something that was intensely alive in the first Christian
> centuries up until the fourth century.[4]

This is one side of the ritual. And then there is another side:

As late as in the fourth century, there were philosophers in Greece who worked on bringing the ancient etheric astronomy into harmony with Christianity. From this effort then arose the true Gnosis, which was thoroughly eradicated by later Christianity, so that only a few fragments of the literary samples of this Gnosis have remained.

This unification of etheric astronomy with Christianity is especially to be found in the School of Dionysius the Areopagite. And what appeared as Gnosis around this school was wiped out completely by Christianity in the later centuries.

We can understand that all this wisdom slowly came to an end when thinking developed in such a way that any kind of spiritual knowledge was gradually wiped out: the curtain of the fourth century came down. And then in the sixth century – in the year 533 – for the first time the teachings of Dionysius were written down. These writings were then preserved in small circles of Christian teachers; they came, for instance, centuries later to the one we know as Scotus Erigena. Scotus Erigena was deeply moved by the writings of Dionysius, translated them into Latin and wrote a commentary on them. And then some four centuries later they reached Albertus Magnus and Thomas Aquinas. The introduction to the commentary of Dionysius by Thomas Aquinas shows in what high regard these great teachers still held Dionysius.

From history it is known that until about the middle of the sixth century the philosophy schools in Athens continued to combine Gnostic wisdom – the old etheric astronomy – with the new Christianity. But in the sixth century something special happened. In exactly the same year as the teachings of Dionysius were written down, another document was issued which was of the greatest importance and which still works right into our time. This was the *Codex Justinianus,* a comprehensive code of Roman law containing innumerable court proceedings and imperial decisions for every possible walk of life. The sixth century was dominated by the reign of Emperor Justinian in Byzantium from 527 to 564, accompanied by his wife Theodora. Before she became empress she was a well-known prostitute and actress. She was a very interesting woman. She did a great deal of social work, she founded the first maternity hospital – probably because she was a prostitute. She was the power behind Justinian. During these thirty years – the middle of the sixth century – Justinian ruled over the greater part of Europe. Under him the might and power of the Roman Empire was regained.

At his side were two generals – rather dark figures – Narses and Belisarius who carried out Justinian's ambition of reconquering large parts of the Western Roman Empire. In 526 Theoderic the Great, king of the Ostrogoths, died in Ravenna, allowing Justinian's general to conquer the Ostrogoth kingdom. Belisarius reconquered Carthage and large parts of North Africa, from the east the Pannonian Avars invaded, and in the north there was fighting with the kingdom of the Franks or Merovingians who killed each other – sons, uncles, aunts, children and grandchildren. It was a century of blood, a century of hatred, a century of revenge. In my personal opinion, all its ups and downs, all its fights and battles, gave rise to the different parts of the Song of the Nibelungs, which was written down much later. It is unimaginable what went on under the impact of unbridled Teutonic and Germanic blood-letting. It was almost a war of all against all that took place during this sixth century across the whole of Europe.

And another thing took place during this sixth century. The sun of Irish Christianity started to shine over the whole of Europe. Columba, born in 527, and his pupil Columbanus, born in 543, began their astonishing mission of the Irish monks across northern and western Europe at the beginning of the seventh century. Around the same time, in 570 Muhammad was born in Arabia, and at the beginning of the seventh century the Islamic conquests began.

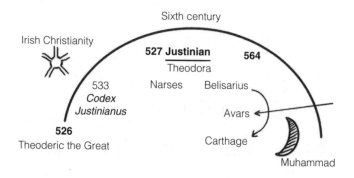

In this time the last remnant of primeval wisdom in the form of the teachings of Dionysius the Areopagite were written down, circulated and read – perhaps by only a very few, but they were read. Perhaps we can imagine that between these two powers there started to grow, to sprout, the last remnant of the primeval wisdom, in the form of the writings of Dionysius the Areopagite. In the same century the last philosophers of Athens were expelled by Justinian. Several of the great fathers of the Church like Origen were declared heretics. The last residue of spirituality was gone. But the sun began to shine in the west, while the first signs of an opposition to spirituality arose in the east with Islam.

4

Central Europe, Threefolding and the Grail

Lecture 4,
Sunday, April 8, 1962

In the last lecture we tried to go one step further in describing and understanding the images of the first centuries following the Mystery of Golgotha. It is strange and puzzling to see how the central event of the whole evolution of our planetary existence did not appear to have more fundamental repercussions in outer history. The Roman Empire simply continued to begin with, in all its glory. Even a few decades after Jerusalem had been the centre of all history, physical and spiritual, the Emperors of Rome destroyed the city, burned the temple and eradicated most of what had been the stage of the acts of Christ. The mysteries, under the guardianship of the Roman Empire, lived on; the mysteries in the Near East continued to exist and to initiate hundreds and thousands of people. The wisdom of the Greeks continued. Stoicism developed; the Epicurean philosophies spread as if nothing had happened. So it appears. Humanity continued as if the Mystery of Golgotha had not occurred. Only very gradually, from one century to the next, a certain impact is made.

We heard Rudolf Steiner's description of two spiritual streams which were flowing during the first three centuries from the east to the west. The first was the remnants of the mysteries, the rituals of the Mithraic mysteries, spreading up the Danube and across more and more of Europe from the east to the west. And in the south, the second stream flowed along the borders of North Africa, taking in the islands of the Mediterranean, Rhodes, Crete, Sicily, Sardinia, as well as parts of southern Italy and Spain. This wisdom gradually spread as the *etheric astronomy,* the astronomy that still contained the archetypal wisdom, which did not describe the outer course of the planets nor the geometry of the stars, but contained knowledge of all the beings who permeate the whole cosmos.

Increasingly during these first few centuries, within the stream of the Mithraic mysteries, the awareness gradually grew that Mithras was only the forerunner of the Christ, that in the ritual of Mithras the Christ himself would have to replace Mithras who had been worshipped until now. On the other hand, in the different centres where etheric astronomy was taught, where the Gnosis survived as the wisdom of a few, there was the will and the longing to unite with the Christian impulse and with all the spiritually shining through the Mystery of Golgotha.

The fathers of the Church still carried a certain amount of Gnostic wisdom, but were also deeply connected with the Mithraic mysteries, for instance in all that lived in Arianism. But in the fourth century, more or less at a stroke, that all disappeared. It was destroyed through the fact that the Roman Empire instigated Christianity as the state religion. Constantine the Great (who founded Constantinople) destroyed all the spirituality from the east that still tried to permeate the developing continent of Europe. And like an epitaph of what happened in this fourth century, we can look at the figure of Julian the Apostate, trying in vain to fight against the eradication of all spirituality, but who was murdered and in this moment spirituality as it was living in the East more or less came to an end.

Then we came to the sixth century and the description of the main events of this most important historical period. What I described was more or less true for all the region south of the Danube – for the whole of the south of Europe, the Mediterranean part of the European continent. But in the north, in the parts which today are Poland, the western parts of Russia, Germany, northern France, and also in Britain, there was this tremendous migration of peoples and tribes. Wave after wave came from the East. This migration lasted for several centuries. From the distant and nearer parts of Asia there came – as if out of a bottomless well – millions of Germanic and later Slav peoples who gradually pushed westward and settled in Europe. You have to grasp all this to understand the sixth century. Against this background we spoke about certain events of the sixth century, particularly of the year 533 when the esoteric teaching of Dionysius the Areopagite was written down and became available to anyone who could read.

If we try to find the three 33-year periods of this sixth century, they can be clearly distinguished. The first is from 495 until 528. This is the period when the kingdom of Theoderic in Italy disintegrated, it is the time when the migration of the people, after having invaded the western part of the Roman Empire, was crushed for the last time.

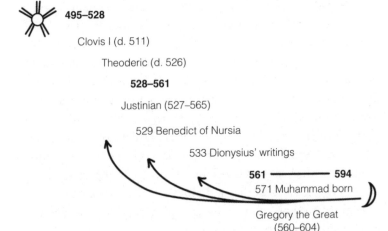

495–528

Clovis I (d. 511)

Theoderic (d. 526)

528–561

Justinian (527–565)

529 Benedict of Nursia

533 Dionysius' writings

561 ————— **594**

571 Muhammad born

Gregory the Great
(560–604)

Then comes the period from 528 until 561. This period coincides with the reign of the Emperor Justinian. For the last time the whole of the Roman Empire tried to shine again, like a candle flaring up before it burns out. During this second period the *Codex Justinianus* was published. The Athenian philosophers were driven away, the councils of Rome were extinguished. Byzantium as well as Rome formed one Empire, extending into Spain, reaching out into the north of Africa, where the Vandal kingdom was destroyed and conquered. For the last time Rome shone. But it was no longer light, but uttermost destructive darkness which emanated from it. And within this darkness, like a tiny little flame, there remained the *Urweltweisheit,* the primeval wisdom in the writings of Dionysius the Areopagite.

Then came the last period from 561 to 594. This is the period when the Roman Church for the first time in its history started to take hold of outer events, started to make itself felt as a worldly power. Pope Gregory the Great, who through Augustine Christianised England, established Christianity as a kingdom on earth, as a kingdom that he ruled. And from the east, Islam began to rise. Muhammad was born round about 570, and his power grew like the waxing moon.

If we try to understand what has happened in these three 33-year periods, I would not hesitate to say that a central theme was that Theoderic was unable to conquer the kingdom of the Franks. Although Clovis, the founder of this kingdom, had died and his sons murdered each other, this kingdom of the Franks started to take shape. In the middle period which saw the last powerful appearance and sudden decay of the Roman Empire, something else was born. This is the central part of Europe, as a first seed of what, hundreds of years later, became Germany. And I don't mean today's political entity, I mean simply Central Europe, including Austria and even Scandinavia. At the same time through Gregory, Augustine, and others, England came into being.

The first archetypal image of the future Europe began to take shape. It is like an embryo, in its very early stages, which already delineates the later France, Germany and England, in which the destiny of Europe could start to incarnate in stages. I deliberately express it in this way when I say in which the destiny of Europe could start to incarnate. Because this destiny is a being that seeks to express itself as individuality in this melting-pot of a developing Germany. It also forms the vessel of the consciousness soul, which England should bear, and also expresses itself in the mind-soul, the intellectual soul, in the region of France. This is the threefold being of Europe's destiny, which in these three steps in the sixth century begin to take shape. It begins to indicate in which direction it should go; it begins, as it were, to formulate itself.

I am trying to describe it so that we can really feel what it means that an entirely new world is born. It is so easy to say 'Europe develops', but *how* does it develop? How does Europe really come into being? The fourth century pushed back towards the east the two streams of ritual and of the Gnosis, in order that through this threefold beginning the three different peoples could fulfil their future task to create and represent Europe. Just in this middle period, in 529 and in 533, two great Christian events took place. In 533, as was mentioned earlier, the esoteric teachings of Dionysius was written down, and in 529 something happened which is perhaps of equal importance. The monk Benedict of Nursia founded the first Benedictine monastery at Monte Casino. This event should be inscribed with golden letters into the history of the development of Europe, because with it the first truly European monastery was founded. From then on for at least seven, eight or more centuries the monasteries carried the learning and a great amount of the spiritual substance of Europe within their walls.

Throughout this time, from the west towards the south-east, came the glory of Irish Christianity, and from the east the stream of Muhammad and the Arabs. To be more precise Islam spread along North Africa, and gradually tried through Sicily, through Spain, and even through Crete, to enter and permeate Europe.

What is taking place in these days, the war in Algeria between France and the Muslims, is nothing but the last remnants of what happened in the seventh, eighth and ninth centuries. Only if we see it against this background will we understand why it is being fought in such a ferocious, terrible and unimaginable way. And the reason is that Europeans still think they have to defend themselves outwardly against something which inwardly for a long time has already conquered them. Because Europeans are unable to understand how their thinking, their science and so much else has an Arabian source, they try to fight outwardly what inwardly they are not any more able to overcome.

We can see the gesture of the streams of Arab Islam coming from the south, wanting to surround this growing child of Europe. Against this, Irish Christianity started from within, from certain places where it had established itself, to permeate the uncultured peoples who at that time lived with the light, with the wisdom, with the tender being of Central Europe. We can see the difference: how two opposing elements began to give shape to this developing continent: Irish Christianity tried to establish from within the forces (or certain forces) of the heart; and the intellect of Arabism tried to surround, to enclose, all that Europe should become.

Thus between those two streams, the history of Europe unfolded from the sixth to the ninth century. There are other outer events that are not so important. During this time the Carolingians increasingly assume power over the realm of the Franks, that Charlemagne began to rule, conquering Central Europe and then dividing his empire into three parts, again showing its threefold existence. But essentially, behind the scenes of outer history, it is these two streams that are at work. Think how time and again the Moors were repelled, how Charles Martel and others tried to force the Muslims back into Spain, or even to drive them out of Spain back into North Africa, in order to give the child Europe the possibility to develop and unfold.

Two streams had disappeared: the stream of Gnosis and the stream of the mysteries. Rudolf Steiner described what remained. He showed how in Greece the human self, the ego, was so alive, was so mobile that it still filled everything which was around human beings at that time. But these surviving streams of which I spoke then had to disappear:

> All knowledge that would have been capable of producing a deeper comprehension of Christianity gradually withdrew back into Asia, all insight that could have brought about a [ritual] in which the Christ Triumphant would have appeared rather than [the Christ] who is overwhelmed by the burdens of the cross, whose triumph can only faintly be surmised behind the shadow of the Crucifix. For the Occident, this ebbing away of the wisdom and the ancient ceremonial worship was initially a matter of securing the ego. From the robust force dwelling in the barbaric peoples of the north, the impulse emerged that was intended to supply the power to attach the ego to the earthly human organism.
>
> While this was happening in the regions around the Danube, somewhat south of there, and in southern and western Europe, Arabism was transplanted from the Orient in forms differing from those of the earliest Oriental wisdom. Arabism then made its way as far as Spain, and southwestern Europe became inundated by a fantastic intellectual culture. This was a culture that in the external field of art could not achieve anything more than the arabesque, since it was incapable of permeating the organic realm with soul and spirit. Thus, in regard to the [ritual] ceremonies, Europe was filled, on the one hand with the narration of purely factual events; on the other hand, it was engrossed in a body of abstract, fantastic wisdom that, entering Europe by way of Spain, turned in filtered form into the culture of pure intellect.

What he said was that the Gnosis, the etheric astronomy was now replaced by intellectuality, by the dramatic intellect which the Arabs brought into Europe. But what the ritual should have been – a ritual that would have made it possible to see or divine something behind the outer events of the Mystery of Golgotha – this became nothing but a simple narrative of Christ's life on earth.

In this melting-pot of the Germanic races in Central Europe the crude powers of the human ego now tried to direct people's bodily and earthly nature, blood and revenge, and tribal wars still held sway. It is most important to see that there Christianity could only take hold of the hearts of men as an outer fact. The Germanic peoples, the northern people, were told how Christ's life, of the kind of miracles he performed, of how he stilled the storm and how he ruled the waves, of how he healed the sick and made the deaf hear and the blind see. And then how he consented to die on the cross, though he was the greatest ruler of all humankind. During this period people were unable to understand more.

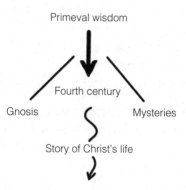

And from the other side, from the south, there came Aristotelian natural science, Aristotelian philosophy in the garment of Arab intellectualism. If we picture this vividly, we will begin to form an impression of these later centuries – the seventh, eighth and ninth centuries. Then out of nowhere, and yet from somewhere, gradually something new arose. Rudolf Steiner describes how in a few people, single ones here and there, something began to dawn. (He does not say so, but in my own opinion, probably most of them had been touched by the wonder of Irish Christianity.)

> In their souls a feeling dawned that there is a lofty
> Christian mystery, the full significance of which is so
> great that the highest wisdom cannot penetrate it; the
> most ardent feeling is not strong enough to develop
> a fitting ceremonial worship for it. Indeed, they felt
> that something emanated from the cross on Golgotha
> that would have to be comprehended by the highest
> wisdom and the most daring feeling. Such ideas arose
> in a few individuals. Something like the following
> profound imagination arose in them. In the bread of
> the Last Supper, a synthesis of sorts was contained, a
> concentration of the force of the outer cosmos that
> comes down to the earth together with all the streams
> of forces from the cosmos, penetrating this earth,
> conjuring forth from it the vegetation. Then, what has
> thus been entrusted to the earth from out of the cosmos,
> in turn springs forth from the earth and is synthetically
> concentrated in the bread and sustains the human body.[2]

What Rudolf Steiner described here is the gradual dawning in a few people that there was something more behind the Mystery of Golgotha, in the time of the ninth century. And then Rudolf Steiner described a second mystery:

> This other mystery, which was linked to the mystery of
> the bread, was the mystery of the holy vessel in which
> Joseph of Arimathea had caught the blood flowing
> down from Christ Jesus. This was the other aspect of
> the cosmic mystery. Just as the bread was regarded a
> concentrated extract of the cosmos, so the blood was

regarded as the extract of the nature and being of man.
In bread and blood – of which wine is merely the outer
symbol – this extract expressed itself for these European
sages. They had truly stepped forth as if out of the
hidden places of the mysteries.

These two images started to live within the souls of people
at that time. Outwardly, out of nowhere, this began to unfold.
Gnosticism was banished into the East and disappeared. The
mysteries of Mithras were rejected and also disappeared, but
they revealed themselves in a new form. Bread is the extract of
all Gnostic wisdom, blood is the symbol for all that will find
expression in a renewed ritual of the mysteries. And now we can
see how the first images of the Holy Grail arose within human souls.

In the sixth century Europe was freed from the past. Old
forms were destroyed and the first seeds of a coming Europe in
its threefold form of England, France and Germany began. But
spiritually nothing was present. In the course of the following
centuries the Arabs tried to bring intellectualism to Europe, and
Christianity was reduced to nothing more than a story of outer
facts. This lasted for three centuries. Then in the ninth century this
process started which has just been described. We can imagine that
this lasted another three centuries. Through the tenth, eleventh
and twelfth centuries more and more the images of the Grail
begin to grow within the human soul. Bread and wine or body and
blood revealed their meaning in various forms. After this, almost
suddenly as if after long winter months, a flower opened and the
different great epics of the Grail appeared. Within a few decades,
from about 1180 to 1220 or 1230, Robert de Boron, Chrétien de
Troyes and Wolfram von Eschenbach wrote down what for the
last centuries had lived, grown and taken shape in human souls. I
would like to say only a few brief words about these three different
presentations of the Mystery of the Holy Grail.

Robert de Boron describes the story of Joseph of Arimathea
and the story of the actual Grail. Joseph of Arimathea brought the
cup which had held the blood of Christ from the east to the west.

He went to England, bringing the cup to the north-west of Europe. And around this cup the world of the deeds of the Knights of King Arthur was established. If we look carefully at Robert de Boron's account, we find that he describes Joseph of Arimathea as an old man. There are two versions. In the one Emperor Vespasian, when he conquered Jerusalem, found Joseph of Arimathea imprisoned in a deep tower where he had been guarding the Grail for the last 35 years. And in the other version an officer of Vespasian's son Titus found a very old man imprisoned in a hidden room, surrounded by a great number of manuscripts on which was inscribed the genealogy of the leading generations of the whole of mankind, from the beginning until that time. And the officer took this old man and his manuscripts by ship to the south of England.

What is it that Robert de Boron described? The Grail is cup containing the whole memory of all mankind which is written in the manuscripts: the spiritual past, the spirit-recollection, of all that once passed. And this journeyed in a hidden way from the East, where the old temple had been destroyed, to be planted into the developing European continent.

Then there is Chrétien de Troyes' book. He focuses on Parsifal, and the Grail remains entirely in the background. He describes Parsifal in images, and we follow Parsifal through different trials, but Parsifal never reaches the Grail. Where did Chrétien get his story from? He claims to have received it from his superior, Philip of Flanders. And describing Philip of Flanders he said that Philip asked no-one except his own free and pious heart, which advised him to do good.

Philip of Flanders is the embodiment of a man who does not ask anyone else but only his free and pious heart. This is conscience. Here we suddenly have something new beginning to dawn. We can say that Parsifal, in the way he is described by Chrétien de Troyes, bears human conscience.

And then we come to Wolfram von Eschenbach. Where did his story come from? Wolfram speaks of his teacher Kyot (or

Kiot), telling us that in Seville Kyot found an old manuscript written in strange letters, and that this manuscript contained the wisdom of Kyot's teacher. This man was Flegetanis, who lived, so Wolfram's epic says, at the time of King Solomon. He had a Jewish mother and a heathen father. In the Old Testament there was a man at the time of King Solomon who had a Jewish mother from the tribe of Naphtali and a Phoenician father. This man was Hiram. There can be no doubt that Flegetanis is the same as Hiram who built the two pillars of Jachin and Boaz in Solomon's temple, and who cast the brazen sea. Hiram represented all that we called the *Urweltweisheit,* the primeval wisdom. So through Hiram or Flegetanis and Kyot the stream flowed from which Wolfram von Eschenbach composed the story of Parsifal and the Holy Grail.

These are the sources of the three stories which gradually formed the image of the Holy Grail. In Robert de Boron Joseph of Arimathea, bearing the memory of the past, came from the Holy Land to the south of England and encountered the Arthurian stream. Then In Chrétien de Troyes we meet the striving human being, Parsifal, the one who acts out of the strength of his conscience. And in Wolfram's version of the story, conscience and memory flow together, so that the *Urweltweisheit,* archetypal wisdom, can again incarnate.

Robert de Boron points to England; Chrétien de Troyes is himself a Frenchman; Wolfram is German. The three parts of the emerging destiny of Europe begin to form, permeated by this entirely new Christian impulse, by these new images of the Grail and of Parsifal. This enabled the *Urweltweisheit* to reappear in a renewed form to prepare for what Europe was to become. In this way we can try to pave a way for an understanding of how history has unfolded, and how we have to look back, in order to understand our own destiny in the twentieth century.

5

The Path of Wisdom through History

Lecture 5,
Thursday, April 12, 1962

What is the reality of the Grail of which Wolfram von Eschenbach said, 'There is a thing; it is the Grail'? I do not think we will be able to give an answer, but we must be able to ask this question, because the images alone will leave us without the substance of reality, which we need to begin to know. The other question I want to explore is about the connection between Paul and the Grail.

We must return again to the primeval wisdom, and hear again from the basic lecture with which Rudolf Steiner introduced his lecture cycle on the spiritual hierarchies. There he speaks fundamentally about the the path of this primeval wisdom through the course of human history. And I will quote a few remarks of Rudolf Steiner where he spoke of the time before Christ:

> Yet, this sublime wisdom was preserved and could always
> be found in certain small circles guarding the mysteries ...
>   This primeval divine wisdom, which streamed
> over humanity in ancient times, was transmitted by

Zarathustra and his pupils, the Chaldean and Egyptian
teachers. It streamed into the Mosaic revelation and
came forth again with a new impulse, as if renewed in
a rejuvenating fountain, in the earthly appearance of
Christ. But following Christ's appearance – that is since
the time of the outward proclamation of Christianity,
indeed as a result of it – the stream of primeval world
wisdom became so deep, so inward in character, that it
could flow into humanity again only gradually.[1]

This is the second step. This primeval wisdom permeated
the third post-Atlantean period (Chaldea and Egypt), and was
rejuvenated by Christianity. And then Rudolf Steiner described
how this wisdom was written down in the Gospels.

Its message may be found in the Gospels and in other
Christian writings that contain the wisdom of the holy
Rishis in a form that has been renewed in a rejuvenating
fountain.

Out of this new well, out of this fresh fountain, there flowed
the four gospels, there flowed the Christian writings, but people
were quite unable to understand them.

The treasures lying in the shafts of Christian revelation,
which are none other than the treasures of Eastern wisdom
(except that they were born from restored powers) were
preserved in narrow circles, and subsequently prolonged in
various mystery societies, such as the Brotherhood of the
Holy Grail, and the Brotherhood of the Rosicrucians.

Here for the first time Rudolf Steiner described the
Brotherhood of the Holy Grail as belonging to the few who were
the guardians and keepers of the renewed holy mysteries, of the
renewed primeval wisdom.

It is important to understand this with a certain degree of
clarity and to treat it earnestly. We are so used to saying, 'Oh
well, I know this, why do you talk again about such things which

are so obvious?' I do so, dear friends, because we can never become sufficiently conscious of the change that took place at the turning-point of time. We must learn to understand the difference between the Holy Spirit before and after the Mystery of Golgotha. The primeval wisdom that came from the west to the east and returned again from the east to the west, is the pre-Christian Holy Spirit. It is this what in the Eastern Church is still called Holy Sophia and is described in many different ways and forms, in images and poems. It is the leading spirit which descended and endowed human existence with knowledge. But this came to an end. It came to an end during the turning-point of time. It came to an end in the time before the Mystery of Golgotha and in early Christian times.

The whole struggle in the following centuries – the darkness, the turmoil, the chaos, the increasing troubles of humanity in Europe – was, is and will be nothing but the struggle to regain the new Holy Spirit; to regain what for most of people is nothing else but a name, the 'Holy Spirit'. We have to grasp this fundamental change from what it once was to what it has now become. In the eastern world, clairvoyance in one or another way is a matter of course and natural, even today – though no longer as widespread as before the Mystery of Golgotha. Then people saw the world around them immediately realising and experiencing the Spirit. No flower, no animal, no tree, no cloud, nothing was without its immediate spiritual reality. Every well and every field had its spirit. Every forest, every tree, everything was filled with spiritual experience. This was such an intense experience that people lived in a twofold, threefold, manifold world that was filled with spirit, and out of this spirit certain forms crystallised as physical objects. That was their everyday experience.

What made it possible that people had this immediate experience of the spirit? This experience was possible through the blood. At birth every human being was endowed, as it were, with a cup of blood given to him out of the ocean of humankind. This was the gift received at birth. And with this blood each person was not only a child of his parents, members of the tribe, but was a member of humanity. And in being members of humanity they were carriers of clairvoyant wisdom. They carried this wisdom, but not as knowledge: they carried it as immediate beholding, as immediate experience. It was the blood which, so to speak, reflected this experience, as Rudolf Steiner described it:

> Knowledge of the supersensible, of the spirit-and-soul, was dependent in olden times on the blood: the blood coursing through the human being itself brought the revelation into the material world ... Formerly this was possible, because the blood itself was the bearer of supersensible knowledge. The event of Golgotha enable people of good will to be free of this dependence; but the general trend of evolution was such that for a time people continued the once well-founded habit in regard to the blood. They no longer bore within themselves the blood which reveals the divine, yet they still wanted to understand the divine and spiritual through their own innate attributes.[2]

Once blood had been the carrier of supersensible wisdom, of clairvoyant knowledge, but this gradually had to come to an end and something else had to take its place. This is one of the great deeds of Paul: that he as a Jew was the first to point to this very fact.

I mentioned earlier how every well, every field, every cloud, how everything was endowed with its very own spiritual being. And of course every nation – insofar as nations existed at that time – every people had their very own mythology, because it had it own special spiritual experiences. This was different in different parts of the world. But one people were an exception: these were the Jewish people, because the Israelites were convinced that they were the chosen people and that their God was the God of the whole of humankind. This was the case in pre-Christian times (and has not really changed since). Paul understood this through his initiation at Damascus where he learned something entirely new:

For Paul was the first to declare that neither blood nor identity of race, nor any factor by which human knowledge had been determined in pre-Christian times, could remain, but that man himself must establish his relation to knowledge through *inner* initiative: that there must be a community of those whom he designated as Christians, a community to which people would ally themselves in spirit and soul, rather than being placed into it by their blood, one which they would choose to belong to.

Rudolf Steiner's words here are of the greatest importance. We see that Paul was the first to understand that the archetypal wisdom came to an end for one reason only: that the bonds of blood-relationship also came to an end. The cup of blood, which all people received when they were born, lost its importance. The mystical powers of the blood gradually disappeared, and with these clairvoyance came to an end, and humanity became poor, empty and barren. Paul went through this experience. He tried to overcome this emptiness through persecuting the followers of Christ. But through the experience at Damascus, he learned that something entirely new was to dawn within humanity.

Here lies the root of the connection of Paul to the Holy Grail, because one part of the Holy Grail is the mystery of the blood. It was altogether due to the disappearance of the mystical powers of this very special fluid that the mystery of blood could dawn within the human soul. Paul was the one who was able to point this out.

This is the one thing. But something else happened parallel to this change in the condition and constitution of the blood. Rudolf Steiner described how the impulse of the Christ after the Mystery of Golgotha started to work in the unconscious part of the human soul. Rudolf Steiner described the Battle of Rome in the fourth century, where in a dream Constantine is told that he would be victorious if he carried a banner with the monogram of Christ inscribed on it. Steiner described this as a work of the Christ impulse in the depths of the human soul:

> Truly, like a stream which has disappeared into mountain cavities, so that it is no longer to be seen up above and one may form the strangest conjectures about it, so the Christ Impulse works on below the surface – works, at first, as occult, i.e. hidden, reality.

And as soon as you read further, you are suddenly faced with a kind of confession which Rudolf Steiner makes:

> My dear friends, allow me at this point to confess to you that when in my occult researches I tried to follow this stream, I often lost trace of it; I had to search for places where it reappeared.[3]

That means there is a hidden stream within the human soul unknown, so to speak, outwardly, historically. But time and again it comes to the surface, and when this happens – as we can read if we follow up what Rudolf Steiner described here – it appears in connection with the Holy Grail.

This is the second thing which we have here to take into account. First, there is the stream of blood which comes to an end: clairvoyance dies out and the renewal came about through Paul. Then there is this hidden stream within the human soul (not in the blood, but in the human soul), and this reappears as Parsifal's search for the Holy Grail. Now, in an entirely new way, we come again to the mystery of wine and the mystery of bread which we discussed in the last lecture.

But now the great question is, where is the primeval wisdom? Have we lost it altogether? I think that some kind of answer is possible, which I give very tentatively. In the first lecture of the cycle *The East in the Light of the West* held in the important year 1909, Rudolf Steiner opened with the question, what is the Holy Grail? He described one of the legends of the Grail that tells how, out of the crown of Lucifer, a stone fell down; out of this precious stone a cup was formed, and into this cup the blood of the Christ was received:

> Out of the stone which fell from Lucifer's crown was
> made the Holy Grail. This precious stone is in a certain
> respect nothing else ... than the full power of the Ego.[4]

Of course such a thing is said quite easily. But what do we really mean if we try to grapple with this image that the human self or ego is the stone formed into a cup, which received the blood of Christ?

We must immediately think of Paul and of his experience, 'Not I, but Christ in me.' We must learn to understand the connection between 'I' and 'Christ in me' which is no longer based on blood-ties. Otherwise we shall not even be able to make the first step towards an understanding of the legends, and through the legends of the mysteries, and through the mysteries the reality of the Holy Grail. We are dealing with something totally new, something quite fundamental: the power of the blood has gone. With regard to knowing and knowledge we are no longer part of the humankind. The ocean, the sea of the blood, has lost its power. Historically, the moment when this happened was when the blood from the cross entered the earth. And the light which started to shine from this new blood, could start to fill the cup of the developing human self or ego. In this way the occult power of the Christ impulse worked in the subconscious depths of the human soul.

But all this is preparation to receive the message which emanates from what, in many different forms and ways, and in many images, is the Holy Grail. If we now ask where and when and how did the Mystery of the Grail start in the first place, then, in the last lecture of the same cycle, we can find something that I offer as a kind of explanation. Because in this last lecture Rudolf Steiner spoke quite suddenly about one of the great primeval teachers of mankind, of one of the greatest initiates, Skythianos.

> Among the great initiates who had founded mystery
> places in the west for the preservation of the old Atlantean
> wisdom, a wisdom that entered deeply into all the secrets
> of the physical body, was the great Skythianos, as he was

called in the Middle Ages. And anyone who knows the
nature of the European mysteries knows that Skythianos is
the name given to one of the greatest initiates of the earth.

Skythianos was the guardian of the age-old primeval
Atlantean wisdom. He was the keeper of what we could call
the pre-Christian Holy Spirit. And then Steiner described how
Skythianos, together with two others – Buddha and Zarathustra
(let me call these three Bodhisattvas) – were called together by
one who was still higher than they, by Manes.

> It is said that a few centuries after Christ had lived on
> earth, there was held one of the greatest assemblies of the
> spiritual world connected with the earth that ever took
> place, and that there Manes gathered round him three
> mighty personalities of the fourth century after Christ.
> In this figurative description a most significant fact in
> connection with spiritual development is expressed.
> Manes called these persons together to consult with
> them as to the means of reintroducing the wisdom that
> had lived throughout the changing times of the post-
> Atlantean age and of causing it to unfold more and more
> gloriously in the future.[5]

We see it was not just a matter of preserving the primeval
wisdom, but how it could be renewed to live more strongly into
the future. Here we find the founding, the source of the Holy
Grail. When Christianity became the state religion of the Roman
Empire, when Constantine became Emperor, when Julian the
Apostate was murdered and knowledge of the spiritual sun
was extinguished, when the mystery temples were closed, the
mysteries were stamped out and Gnosis declared heretical and
forbidden, then an assembly of some of the greatest initiates was
held, and the Holy Grail was instituted, as the mystery of the
coming Europe.

It was instituted in such a way that we can now see the
following in a kind of picture. Primeval wisdom continued

to the time of the Mystery of Golgotha, then parted into two streams that gradually disappeared – the stream of Gnosis and the stream of the mysteries. And what was left, in the centre, were the gospels, which told the story of the events in the Holy Land. But the mysteries slowly reappeared behind the scenes of outer history, as the mysteries of the Grail. They appeared, for instance, in tenth, eleventh and twelfth centuries with the Cathars, and in the thirteenth, fourteenth, fifteenth centuries in the great brotherhood of the Rosicrucians. That is the one stream. The other stream is the Gnosis, leading from Dionysius the Areopagite to Scotus Erigena and further to Thomas Aquinas. Then all these streams gradually dried up.

Out of the stream which related the events of the Gospel there arose what we know today as Protestantism. Out of the stream of Gnosis there gradually evolved the dogmatic teaching of Roman Catholicism. And from the mysteries the stream of esoteric Christianity remained – until, at the beginning of the twentieth century, something entirely new came through anthroposophy.

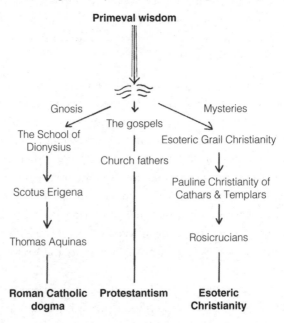

This gives us an impression of the connection between these various events. But I would also like to give another matter in a kind of picture. We spoke of Skythianos, Buddha, Zarathustra, and the great Manes. These four who held the assembly that led to the revelation of the Grail. In most of the Grail stories you can find them as Titurel, Amfortas, Trevrezent and Parsifal. Titurel is the keeper of the primeval wisdom: he built the Castle of the Grail in thirty years, and in this castle enshrined the whole primeval wisdom of humankind. Titurel prepared the cup. Trevrezent is the one who knew that the earth became the body of the Christ, that the blood of Christ transformed the whole sphere of this earth. Amfortas knew that the ancient power of the blood had to die, and that disease and death were the experiences which brought about a possible renewal. Parsifal is the one who knew that the stone which fell out of the crown of Lucifer was the true human self, or ego, and tried to fulfil what Paul knew, 'Not I, but the Christ in me.'

Skythianos
Titurel
Maundy Thursday

Buddha   *Zarathrustra*
Trevrezent   Amfortas
Good Friday   Holy Saturday

Manes
Parsifal
Easter Sunday

Here we can see Easter appearing: as Maundy Thursday, Good Friday, Holy Saturday, and the Sunday of Resurrection. And we can see in connection to each of these days from the Last Supper onwards, four guiding spirits of humanity out of mystery wisdom and how they reappear within the Grail imagery.

In this way a further step is made to approaching the reality of the Grail. It is not just something which happened long ago, which is nice to read about and wonderful to retell. It is something more: it stirs in our blood and beats in our hearts, if we have the courage to experience Easter as a mystery of the whole of humanity.

6

King Arthur and the New Organ of Conscience

Lecture 6,
Thursday, April 17, 1962

In the last lectures we have looked at two streams: the stream of the mysteries and the stream of Gnosis. When they gradually petered out, only one thing was kept alive: the memory of the physical events which had taken place in the Holy Land. The story of Christ Jesus was passed on by word of mouth. And with this story there was also handed over the tale, the image, of the Last Supper. Then something new started to dawn in human souls, which we can describe in the following way. People began to realise that in the Holy Communion something very great and very special, was contained, and a certain kind of intuition appeared: that bread and wine are very special substances, and, as I tried to describe earlier, within the bread the mysteries of the cosmos are contained, whereas in the wine the mysteries of the innermost being of man are to be found. These two – the cosmic and the human aspect of creation, the cosmic and the human aspect of the mysteries – were seen in an entirely new way and began to sprout like a seed within the soul of European humanity. This happened approximately during the fifth and sixth centuries, and then more and more during the ensuing centuries. But also this had an outer reason that it can be seen in a historical picture, which I would like to describe.

The great Church fathers knew that Christianity did not start with the Mystery of Golgotha; for instance they could see that someone like Plato could also be called a Christian philosopher. Or to give another example, if we visit the ruins in Tintagel and read the official guide, we can be struck by the words: 'We find the remnants of a Christian community which lived here during the centuries before Christ.' I don't know what the writer had in mind, but it is true. He could not express it any other way, because he found the remains of a kind of monastery, and therefore said, 'It is a kind of a Christian community.' But these remnants go back many, many centuries before Christ. And these are the relics of what is still today described as the Round Table of King Arthur and his Knights. This is heathen Christianity before the Mystery of Golgotha. From Tintagel a tremendous amount of light and wonder and culture streamed out, not only into this island but onto the Continent, into the regions of France and Northern Europe. This was the one pre-Christian, but Christian, stream which existed.

Rudolf Steiner, in a lecture in London in 1924, described in most wonderful terms the inner life of the Knights of King Arthur; how they lived together with the elements of air and water and warmth, and how cosmic Christianity streamed through these elements and emanated from them. These were the mysteries of the bread, the cosmic mysteries of Christianity, streaming from the north-west of Europe into the south-east. We can write 'King Arthur' or 'the mysteries of bread' in this diagram.

And in the same lecture Rudolf Steiner described how from the east a second stream came, a stream which arose from all that happened during the Mystery of Golgotha – where the Christ himself entered this earth, and where he united himself with the innermost being of man, with the blood and the heart of man. This stream then appears in the fifth, sixth, seventh centuries as the stream of the Holy Grail. All this took place around a great, wonderful personality, named Joseph of Arimathea. And in some of the Grail legends we are told that Joseph of Arimathea came via the Mediterranean, via Africa, via Spain or the south of France (the legends are different) right up to Cornwall and then in Glastonbury established the centre of the Holy Grail during the first centuries after Christ. Here the mysteries of wine, the mysteries of the inner being of man, were celebrated. Let us keep this in mind as a kind of picture.

There are two streams; one from the west and one from the east. These two streams gradually move towards each other – the cosmic Christ and the human Christ: the cosmic wisdom of the bread, and the most intimate knowledge of the human being in connection with the mystery of the wine.

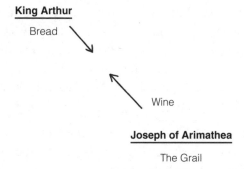

King Arthur

Bread

Wine

Joseph of Arimathea

The Grail

In our last lecture we discussed the further paths of the *Urweltweisheit,* the primeval wisdom. We heard that Rudolf Steiner described how, at the time of the Mystery of Golgotha, something came to an end that until then was of the greatest significance to all people on earth. Until the Mystery of Golgotha, human blood was the organ of all clairvoyance; it was the human blood that reflected in the human soul and the spirit all that was *Urweltweisheit.* At birth, through the blood of the parents people were endowed with the organ of primeval wisdom, of *Urweltweisheit*. They lived embedded in a certain kind of higher knowledge, but gradually, during the centuries before Christ, this came to an end. It was Paul who realised that it was no longer the blood, the bonds of family, tribe and nation that held people together, but that something entirely new had to develop.

Last time I quoted from Rudolf Steiner where he showed that Paul saw that a new community had to start – a community which was not bound by the blood, but a community of knowing, a community of which each individual freely elected to be a part. And this new type of community Paul called 'the Christians'. So we can clearly connect Paul to this new knowledge of the renewal of the human existence. The blood, as the old organ, had come to an end. Knowledge, wisdom, given by blood was no longer possible. Something new had to come about, something which in the course of the centuries to come needed to be born. Human beings would need to strive for this during their life on earth. In the same lecture, Rudolf Steiner pointed out very clearly that in order to bring this about, it was necessary for human beings to become aware of the question of death. Death had to be recognised. And Rudolf Steiner expressed it in the following way:

> In other words, man had to grasp the problem of
> *death,* had to learn that what can be seen of the human
> being here on earth through the senses may perish and
> disintegrate, but that there is within him an entelechy not
> immediately perceptible in this physical frame, a being
> who belongs to the spiritual world. The bond between
> people in this community of Christians was not to be
> dependent on the blood; for the blood, as vitaliser and
> sustainer of that which ends with death, could provide no
> assurance of immortality – although in ancient times the
> spirit and soul shone through it. The spirit and soul

must be revealed in its essence and purity if the
possibility of understanding the problem of death in a
non-materialistic way is not to be lost.[1]

Paul understood that blood was no longer the organ for
primeval wisdom. What was necessary for people to find their
new community of Christians? It was necessary for them to
realise more and more clearly that the body exists, but within
and behind the body there was something greater: the human
spirit-being. But how was that to be achieved? So the question at
that time was how to pierce through the barriers created by the
developing intellect.

After formulating this question, let us turn to something else.
In another series of lectures I tried to approach the question
of memory and conscience.[2] We described the various forms
of memory throughout the evolution of mankind. During the
fourth and fifth centuries before Christ the first beginnings of
the human conscience developed. Then we described the first
appearance of memory, of cosmic memory, which was entirely
bound up with the blood, where individuals, (in so far as they
already were an individual) remembered not only their own
life, but remembered the life of their fathers and forefathers.
During the Lemurian epoch this cosmic memory was simply
mirrored by the blood; it was inscribed in the Akashic Record,
which every human being was able to read at any moment of his
life. There was the organ of the 'third eye', the 'pineal-eye-organ'
which was able to read the script of cosmic memory; everybody
could perceive quite generally and impersonally all that had
happened before his time. Then this cosmic memory faded, and
connected with the process of the developing physical body; the
skull closed, the pineal eye diminished in size, and gradually
became what it is today – this tiny little pineal gland in the centre
of our brain.

Describing these great events, we used the image of Lucifer's
crown, and how out of this crown a precious stone fell down
to earth, and became something which in the legends of the

Holy Grail is described as the cup into which Joseph of Arimathea collected the blood of the Christ on the cross.

This pineal gland is a very special organ. It not only has a very special location, but Rudolf Steiner described it as also having a very special function:

> The brain's etheric body immediately rejects all that comes from the animal kingdom. Indeed, from one part of the brain – one small, ennobled part of the brain – the etheric body also rejects everything that comes from the plant kingdom, and it tolerates only the mineral extract; there, in the vital part of the brain, this mineral extract is united with the purest and noblest radiance entering through the sense organs. Here, the purest, noblest element in light, sound, and warmth encounters the most refined products of the mineral kingdom. The noblest part of the brain is nourished by the union between the most delicate sense impressions and the most refined mineral products.

If you study such a pineal gland under the microscope you will find that normally this tiny little organ, which is no bigger than a dried pea, is filled with the most beautiful calcium crystals which have a form only to be compared to tiny little rose petals. If we read Rudolf Steiner's description we can begin to understand the calamitous consequence if no pure and noble sense-impressions – no sounds, no colours, no warmth, no mineral nourishment – reach this very special organ. And then Rudolf Steiner added the following:

> The legend of the Holy Grail tells us of that miraculous food, prepared from the finest effects of the sense impressions and the finest effects of the mineral extracts, whose purpose is to nourish the noblest part of human beings throughout life on earth. All other nourishment would kill them. This celestial food is contained in the vessel of the Holy Grail.[3]

So here we find another image of the Holy Grail. Every one of us carries this image within ourselves into which the finest and noblest sound, light, mineral substance and warmth gather, and which keep alive the noblest part of ourselves. But what is this noblest part of our whole existence? What is the purpose of this very special organ which the etheric body guards from any other kind of substance and food? This pineal gland is the organ of our conscience. This organ of human conscience, which Steiner connected to the Holy Grail, is an organ that needs to develop more and more in future.

In the fourth and fifth centuries before Christ, conscience started to grow in human souls, but to begin with in only a few, in the most noble ones. Gradually it developed, and Paul was the first to point to conscience in a fully developed way. Time and again you can read how he speaks in his Letters about human conscience. And this human conscience continued to develop. But what is conscience? We can begin to see that conscience is not only an organ of morality, it is the part in our soul which gives us knowledge of ourselves. In Rudolf Steiner's *Theosophy,* we can read his description of the consciousness soul:

> We will call this eternal element that lights up within the soul the consciousness soul ...
>
> But the very core of human consciousness, the 'soul within the soul,' so to speak, is what 'consciousness soul' means here ... We will apply the term 'consciousness soul' to that part of the soul in which truth lives.[4]

We can understand that the consciousness soul, the bearer of spiritual truth, is the bearer of our conscience, and that our conscience is the seat of the consciousness-soul, and that the consciousness-soul is the mother of our conscience. Conscience and consciousness soul are in various forms, in various appearances, one and the same. Our conscience – *Gewissen* in German – is knowledge *(Wissen)* of ourselves.

Our conscience is the consciousness of our existence and is thereby able to judge it. This, in modern words, is what Paul described when he spoke of the blood losing its living, creative possibility for clairvoyant wisdom. Something else had to grow in its place.

And now what had once been the organ of cosmic memory, this tiny seed, which through thousands of years was guarded and gradually developed into the pineal gland, two thousand years ago started to become the organ of the conscience. If we look for a true image of conscience in the consciousness soul, we can, perhaps find nothing more fitting than the image of the Pietà. In the lap of the mother, in the lap of the bride – in the lap of the consciousness soul – there rests the body of the son, the body of the bridegroom, which will rise like conscience in our consciousness-soul.

If we now go back to the legend of the Grail, these two streams – the cosmic wisdom of the bread, and the wine of the knowledge of the human being – united more and more. They united in the ninth century. At that time something entirely new appeared. This was the figure of Parsifal, the son of the widow, who had to go through the veil of darkness, to search for what the growing conscience had to develop within the human soul. Rudolf Steiner once spoke in the following way about King Arthur, the Holy Grail and Parsifal:

> Everything that the sentient soul was to experience through the later mysteries is bound up with the pictorial concepts of King Arthur's Round Table.
>
> What the intellectual soul was to experience in this later time has in turn found legendary form in the saga of the Holy Grail.[5]

Then in Parsifal the consciousness soul starts to dawn and unfold. We could also describe this process in the following way. In the stories of King Arthur's Round Table, we meet something with which humankind at that time was endowed – a kind of dumbness or dullness of existence. The beginning of the new conscience was already there, but it was silent and dull. In this dulled state the Knights of King Arthur knew what was good and what was evil.

Then came the intellectual soul, and with it all that started to permeate human blood and hearts with the Christ impulse. And at that same time, out of this dullness doubt developed, doubt whether a deed was right or wrong, whether the voice of conscience really spoke the truth or simply deceived. Only gradually, out of this doubt, a condition of the soul develops which Wolfram von Eschenbach describes with a word which can hardly be translated: he calls it *Saelde,* clarity of soul. We could also call it the new conscience. These are the three stages of conscience which all merge into the different stories of the Grail: dullness, doubt, and the new conscience.

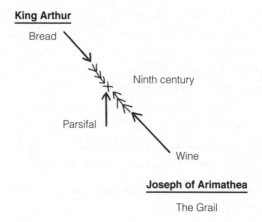

How does Parsifal come to this sudden awakening which makes him search once more for the Castle of the Grail? He meets the bride in whose lap the bridegroom rests. Parsifal recognises the bridegroom as the one who was killed through Parsifal's own misdeeds. This meeting, seeing this image, brought about the awakening of conscience within Parsifal.

So, out of conscience – out of meeting the bridegroom – the consciousness soul was born.

Cosmic memory has died away; Atlantean memory has passed away; rhythmic memory hardly exists any more in us; we have a certain amount of temporal memory, as Rudolf Steiner calls it; our blood has no family bonds any more. But the new conscience is appearing within us. If we look who continued what Paul started two thousand years ago, we can see that the one who continued Paul's work was none other than Parsifal. He searched for the castle of the Grail; He searched for the new conscience; he searched for the ever-renewing power of the spirit. In Novalis' unfinished novel *Heinrich von Ofterdingen,* we can see something beginning to shine that we might call the new conscience:

> 'When,' asked Henry, 'will the need for all fear, all pain, all want, and all evil be removed from the universe?'
>
> 'When there is only one power – the power of conscience. When Nature has become modest and moral. There is only one cause of evil – common weakness; and this weakness is nothing but meagre ethical receptivity, and lack of charm in freedom.'
>
> 'Do please make the nature of conscience comprehensible to me.'
>
> 'If I could do that, I would be God, for conscience arises in the very act of understanding it.'[6]

If we learn to understand conscience, it begins to exist. And then Novalis continued:

> Conscience is the inborn mediator of every human being. It represents the place of God on earth, and hence for so many is the highest and ultimate. But how far removed was that former science, which was called ethics or moral doctrine, from the pure form of this sublime, comprehensive personal thought. Conscience

is man's most individual essence in full transfiguration, the divine primal man.

Novalis says here that the conscience is the mediator of God on earth, that conscience is the organ which so to speak reveals the archetype of human existence. And this, dear friends, is the Grail.

7

Three Stages of Conscience

Lecture 7,
Monday, April 23, 1962

I have the impression that this path which we have followed together to discover the background to the development of memory and conscience can be seen as a fitting contribution to the hundredth anniversary of Rudolf Steiner's birth. To bring a new understanding of memory and conscience was one of his greatest aims, and even one of his last letters to members was about this theme. But today's lecture is not only a conclusion, but also an Easter address.

The last time we were together, we reached a decisive step in our deliberations. I described the consciousness soul as that part of the human soul which is the bearer of our conscience: that it is precisely in the consciousness soul that conscience starts to unfold, so we could say that the consciousness soul is the soul of conscience. And either word is true; either name points to the very nature of this consciousness soul, because within the vast expanse of consciousness, there appears what we may call conscience.

Conscience and consciousness soul also revealed themselves as being identical with that special condition of the human soul which Wolfram von Eschenbach, in his book *Parzival,* calls *Saelde,* which can perhaps be translated as 'clarity of the soul'. It is an inadequate translation, for the word *Saelde* also expresses what is contained in the German word *Seligkeit,* which we may perhaps translate as 'spiritual bliss'. But 'bliss' is also not a very good expression for what is meant here. So what does *Saelde* actually mean? *Saelde* appears in Parsifal; it appears in the human soul; it comes in that moment when the human soul, and especially the intellectual soul and the sentient soul, clear certain parts of their existence in order to make room for the spirit. We may use the image of the full moon. This image shows the intellectual soul and the sentient soul, filled with sensory impressions, filled with feelings, filled with emotions, filled with drives. But as soon as the moon starts to wane, and instead of the soul-content a certain amount of spirit-existence begins to appear within this empty space, the condition of *Saelde* is reached.

Rudolf Steiner, in a meditation which he once gave, expresses it in the following way, *'Die Seligkeit in der die Seele den Geist findet'* – the *Saelde* when the soul begins to acknowledge or to find the spirit. This is *Saelde.* From this we may perhaps also understand why Easter only begins after this starts to happen in the cosmos, after the first full moon after the spring equinox has passed and the spirit begins to grow in the empty space of the waning moon.

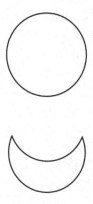

This is the same spirit to which the Christ referred on the first Maundy Thursday, after he had performed the act of consecration of his blood and of his flesh, after he had washed the feet of his disciples and then called them together and then spoke the words which we know from Chapters 14 to 16 of the Gospel of St John. He spoke these words before he went out to Gethsemane and before the events of Good Friday. This also is the same spirit which begins to appear in the human soul when *Saelde* comes about.

But we also saw in the previous lecture, how *Saelde* is only the third stage after the soul had gone through doubt and through dullness. Rudolf Steiner told us that this was the way of Parsifal: to go first through dullness, then to enter the region of doubt, and at last, having gone through these valleys – Percevale, piercing the valley – to reach *Saelde*.

These are the three steps in the development of human conscience. Not only are the steps consecutive, as in Parsifal, but in every one of us there is at the same time, dullness, doubt, and also the first beginnings of *Saelde*. In our sentient soul, dullness is present. In our intellectual soul, we fight with doubt. In our consciousness soul we begin to understand the first glimmer of *Saelde*.

If we follow the life of Parsifal, we find that destiny led him to the castle where he beheld the Grail. He saw all the great events around him: the choir of the knights, the appearing of the Holy Vessel; Amfortas, the ill and suffering Fisher King, the voice of Titurel from high up. But he remained silent and mute – and as we always do, said to himself, 'Tomorrow I will ask.' But tomorrow was too late: when he awoke, the castle was empty; no-one was there any more. The whole revelation had disappeared. He just managed to escape, and then went through the valley of doubt and uncertainty and only gradually did he find his way back to the region of the Grail Castle.

He found his way back under a certain motif – under a motif which I hardly dare mention because the philistines, during the last 150 years, continually quote this saying of Immanuel Kant, when he referred to 'the starry heavens above me, and the moral code within me.' If we take it in its full purity (which not even Kant fully grasped) these two – the stars above and the moral law within the human soul – were what guided Parsifal. Rudolf Steiner described it once in such a way that he inwardly accompanied Parsifal:

> And when I sought to accompany Parsifal in spirit during his return to the Grail, it was often as though there shone forth in the soul how he travelled by day and by night, how he devoted himself to nature by day and to the stars by night, as if the stellar script had spoken to his unconscious self and as if this was a prophecy of that which the holy company of knights who came from the Grail to meet him had said: 'Thy name shines forth in radiance from the Grail.' But Parsifal, quite clearly, did not know what to make of the messages of the stars, for it remained in his unconscious being, and therefore one cannot so very well interpret it, however much one may try to immerse oneself in it through spiritual research.[1]

I quote this because I have the impression that there are few things which are of such importance for our time as this trinity of the consciousness soul, conscience, and the Holy Grail. Because, however we want to walk our inner and outer paths, having the stars above us and the last remnant of the moral code within us, we must see our path in the light of the Grail, the consciousness soul and conscience. An image which unites all three is that of the Pietà, where there is the cup of the moon with the disc of the sun. This is also the image of the bride in whose lap the bridegroom lies. This image speaks to us in the present time, because in the image of the Pietà we are able to find our way towards freedom. This freedom is not meant politically and is in no way connected with the empty phrases which are used in our social life today. Freedom is meant here in the sense of that which Rudolf Steiner called 'spiritual activity' in his book *The Philosophy of Freedom.*

And now we must go back to the point which we reached in the previous series of lectures, when we tried to describe human conscience in its threefold form.[2] I shall briefly recapitulate. There is one part of our conscience that is able to help us, which calls on us, whenever we have lost something and don't know where it is, or forgot entirely to do something that we promised to do. This part of our conscience continually knocks at our consciousness.

Then there is a second part of our conscience which keeps us in equilibrium between having too good a conscience or too bad a conscience. We described a good and a bad conscience as equally wrong: the one tending towards some kind of Luciferic losing oneself, the other tending to Ahrimanic hardening of one's own existence. Only the equilibrium between these two is the real organ of conscience.

And then there is the third one, which is usually referred to as the voice of conscience, which originates in those regions when during sleep we enter the sphere of the Exousiai and Kyriotetes. They accompany us in the morning back into our body, and bring about the voice of conscience, which knocks at the door of our existence.

We are able to trace these three layers, these three great organs of our conscience, in the tenth chapter of the Gospel of St John, when Christ speaks of himself as the Door, as the Good Shepherd, and as being at one with the Father: 'I and the Father are One.'

If we now try to bring this together with what we described as dullness, doubt and *Saelde,* the three stages of the development of conscience. We can see how the voice – as it were the highest form of conscience – calls in the darkness of dullness; how the Good Shepherd tries to maintain equilibrium through the valley of doubt, during all the experiences through which we try to reach the state of *Saelde.* But as soon as we have reached the state of *Saelde*. the Christ speaks to us, 'I am the Door.' And by grace, this door may open and the light of *Saelde* appear within the human soul.

In this way, the manifold form and manifold gestalt of conscience begins increasingly to reveal itself. And we can understand what I mean if I say that conscience and only conscience, and nothing but conscience in the form in which we have tried now to understand it, is the way which leads us towards the Grail.

And now we come back again to the question, where in our physical existence – in the script of the body which the powers of all creation have written – do we find the organ of conscience and its location. We spoke earlier about this very special organ, the pineal gland. We described the pineal gland in its primeval condition, when it was this huge eye which looked out and helped to read the Akashic Record of the memories of the forefathers. Then, when the veil gradually darkened cosmic memory, and the skull closed, this organ shrunk more and more becoming this tiny little thing which it still is today. Rudolf Steiner once described it as an eye of warmth *(ein Wärmeauge)* which looked out into the ether realm and beheld the images of the world.

Last time we again spoke about this organ, describing how this organ at present is nourished by the most noble impressions which stream into us through our ears and eyes, so that only the most refined and beautiful colours, the most subtle sounds and tones, enter this organ. Rudolf Steiner describes this organ as the Holy Grail in us. Of course we read such statements, marvel about them, and then forget them again, because it is so difficult to grasp that each human being has at least the possibility to be the carrier of an imprint of the Holy Grail. What was once long ago the organ for cosmic memory now becomes the organ to which conscience is related. The one has gone, and the other – the new – begins to grow.

Our present-day science has not unlocked the secrets of the pineal gland or revealed its function. Scientists do not know, in spite of thousands of experiments and tens of thousands of investigations, why this organ is there at all. This is not the fault of the scientists: it is the organ itself which does not want to be known, which does not want its name to be revealed. It is still shrouded in a layer of unknowing. But we can begin to understand that this organ is, for instance, intimately connected with our whole warmth system, this warmth which is the carrier of our self or ego. Our ego lives in the body of our warmth, and only within this warmth.

Rudolf Steiner described that precisely in this body of warmth the laws of nature fuse with the laws of morality; that precisely in this body of warmth the human ego stands like the fulcrum connecting natural law and heavenly law.[3] If we take this as an image and see that the pineal gland is the focal point for this body of warmth, then we can understand that in this body of warmth the dullness of our will, the doubt of our feeling, and the *Saelde* of our thinking, start to sprout. So that in the dullness of will, in the doubt of emotions, in the developing clarity or *Saelde* of our thinking, the three organs of conscience rest in the warmth of our existence.

This brings to light things that we discussed earlier. In this new vista we recognise that in this body of warmth – where we can either fulfil or deny the good – there our freedom lies. It is the very same freedom of which I spoke before. Last time we called Parsifal the one who continued what Paul had started. We may go even further and say that what Paul started and Parsifal continued, has in our time come to fulfilment in anthroposophy. I shall quote what, to my mind, is one of the most shattering remarks that Rudolf Steiner ever made. Speaking with the voice of Paul, Steiner said:

> Point the finger at yourself, says Paul, you descended and
> dimmed your vision to such an extent that colour and
> sound do not really appear as something spiritual. You
> believe that colour and sound are something that is there

for you as matter. It is maya. You turned it into maya. You, the human being, have to redeem yourself from that again. You have to obtain again what you forfeited. You descended into matter and now you have to redeem yourself, liberate yourself from that again. But not in the way that Buddha says: vanquish the urge to exist. No, you have to see the existence of the earth in its reality. You have to correct in yourself what you yourself turned into maya. And you can do that by assimilating the power of Christ within yourself which shows you the world in its reality.[4]

These are the words of Paul expressed by Rudolf Steiner for today. Essentially he expressed the same message in the *Philosophy of Freedom,* and in *Truth and Knowledge.* He said the same in very many of his lectures. Actually he repeated this without interruption, trying to fulfil and bring into reality what Paul had known and what Parsifal had gone through. And in doing so a great part of his spiritual investigations were concerned with the discoveries and with the revelation of the nature of conscience. It is precisely this that can be achieved by conscience, and only by conscience.

In the lecture just quoted, Rudolf Steiner spoke about the conscience of the future and how it has to be developed. Every time we do something, good or bad, right or wrong, increasingly the result of what we have sown through our deed will stand before each one of us. We will in future continually be faced by a spirit-image of what later on, in this or in coming lives, will be the fruit of the seed we have sown. We must imagine that this new conscience will develop over centuries and millennia; that this conscience will create as it were the compass of our karma; that this conscience will grow ever greater. It will become, so to speak, the spirit vessel of our existence. What was once cosmic memory has condensed into the organ of the pineal gland. It will in future grow into conscience until it becomes the vessel of our own developing karma. The one has died in order that the other can rise. But this can only rise if it is filled with the Christ impulse, as we have described.

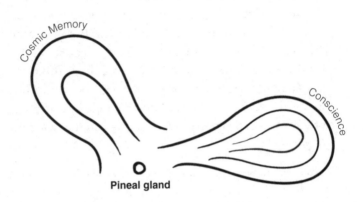

There is a lecture where Rudolf Steiner pointed even more clearly to the organ of this new conscience.[5] He spoke of the human heart within us, and of the pineal gland in the centre of our skull, in the midst of our brain. We can draw it like this.

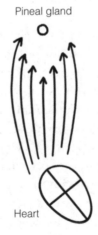

Steiner described how during the day, when we are awake, etheric streams, etheric rays, are continually rising from the heart to the pineal gland. This comes about through what he calls the etherisation of the blood: the substance of the blood within the heart gradually, in a very subtle and fine way, releases ether streams which rise and surround the pineal gland. And then he describes that the same process also takes place macrocosmically, and started in the moment when from the cross, the blood of the Christ entered the earth. From this moment onwards his blood began to radiate its etheric power, its light and substance, into the whole etheric sheath of the earth. This cosmic light, this cosmic etherised blood, can unite with our own organ, and create the new conscience.

What streams upwards there is the power that continually keeps the Grail alive within us. And it is only this which enables us – or will enable us more and more – to behold the spirit of the earth. Rudolf Steiner described the dawn of conscience in man as the creation of this organ whereby people are able gradually to understand the Christ who appeared on earth. The new conscience is the organ which is going to help us to behold the Risen One in the ether realm of the earth. If this happens, the event of Damascus will be fulfilled for many human beings. And we will be able to understand the words that sound from the altar of the Christian Community in the Act of Consecration on Easter Sunday: 'The Comforter of your earth existence walks in the spirit before you.'

This will only be possible if increasingly the new conscience develops, and there is no doubt that this will come about. There is no doubt that time and again we will meet Christ who walks in the spirit before us, beside us, with us, who helps us, guides us, and bestows his love on us.

The Holy Grail

Lectures held in Newton Dee, Aberdeen, 1954

1

Exoteric and Esoteric Christianity

Lecture 1,
Thursday, April 1, 1954

The fourth, eleventh and nineteenth centuries were key times for the decreasing possibility of human beings to behold the spiritual world. In the nineteenth century there were people, firm and strong in their physical existence, but quite unable to behold anything of the spiritual world. For humanity these centuries were quite a special karmic development.

In our present time, mankind has to grow more and more aware of aspects of Rudolf Steiner's spiritual science or anthroposophy. Anthroposophy is not meant for our intellect only, but must be digested like food. It must become living bread and a real necessity for life. We should even feel hungry for meditation within our soul and spirit. Through that we will grow more and more aware of everything around us and within ourselves, and outer events will turn into inner experiences. If we learn to experience the working of the spiritual world upon us, we can become a kind of instrument that various spiritual beings may play. The events of history were brought about by such working of spiritual beings.

The sufferings of First and Second World Wars were not only events here on earth, but spiritual beings experienced themselves in it. Through these events spiritual beings, with the help of human beings, underwent their own development towards good as well as evil. Human history is the lowest form of world history. World history is cosmic evolution. All that we suffer as well as enjoy, is part of this evolution through which the angelic and archangelic beings connected with human beings have to go. They could not work without us. We could not do anything at all without them. We as human beings are one with the third hierarchy. Human beings have to develop their individuality, which is as yet tenuous and feeble. Nothing we do is only due to us, but the *awareness* of all we think, feel and will, this alone is due to us. Everything else is the emanation of spiritual beings.

Out of present events, such as the formation of the North Atlantic Treaty, the division of Central Europe, and so on, the question arises, will Europe be able to discover its present task? The last two thousand years culminating in the twentieth century have seen continuous attempts to build Europe. From a spiritual point of view, all the streams of development flow together and raise the great question, will Europe understand its task? What is the task? The task is that European people learn to understand the path to the Holy Grail. For this Europe was created. Only if the different nations of Europe are able to understand this, will the possibility come to grow out of the present dilemma.

What does the path of the Holy Grail mean? The mystery of the Holy Grail is intimately connected with *bread* and *wine*. Mystery knowledge tells that what bread symbolises contains the mysteries of the macrocosm, and wine contains the mysteries of the microcosm. The history of Europe is nothing but a continuous permeating of everything by the mystery of bread and wine. This took place in two ways. In the outer way bread and wine were used in sacraments at the altar before all people. In the inner way where bread and wine were not used outwardly, but certain human beings tried to penetrate the mysteries behind bread and wine, to perceive their reality as spiritual deeds.

Before Christ, in the fourth post-Atlantean epoch, especially the Greek people carried the development of humanity. Greek culture permeated southern Europe and Asia Minor. The foundations of our present civilisation came from Greek culture: the way of thinking, art, and so on. All that Greece brought about was due to the spiritual being who led Greek culture. It was an archangelic being who – through his deeds was to rise into a higher sphere, up to the status of a Time-Spirit – led the whole epoch. But this archangelic being renounced this rise into a higher sphere, because it intended to take on a different task, and knew that in this sacrifice he would be able to serve in a better way. This being gradually grew to become the leader of exoteric Christianity, which then found its expression especially in the form of the Roman Catholic Church and in the Protestant Church.

The Greek content of the Gospels has a certain amount of spirituality, which is mostly lost in the German, English or Latin translations. In the east another striving remained under the leadership of spiritual beings who did not support the exoteric stream of Christianity. They wanted the worship at the altar imbued with the eastern mysteries, particularly the Mithraic mysteries, coming from Persia over Asia Minor to Europe.

Some of this sacramental stream went over to the west of Europe, especially to Ireland, where something else started to develop around the Mystery of Golgotha. All the western parts of Britain (the west of Scotland, the Isle of Man, Wales, Cornwall), as well as Brittany and the Spanish Pyrenees were inhabited by the Celtic people at the time of Golgotha, and spiritually these parts of Europe were at that time permeated by the stream of the Druids. These were initiates, carrying wisdom which did not regard the coming of the Christ to earth, but regarded Christ as a spiritual being working throughout the etheric sphere with all his power of light and of the Logos. The Celtic people were also led by an archangel. The Celts had to die out, and their guiding being was to rise into a higher sphere. But this being, too, renounced the rising, and in doing so was given the task of leading esoteric Christianity, expressed outwardly in the legends of the Holy Grail and in all that permeated Europe through the stream of Rosicrucianism particularly from the fifteenth and sixteenth centuries.

In the centre of Europe – in the Teutoburg Forest in Germany – there was another pre-Christian mystery centre, the Externsteine. There was the centre for another archangel who inspired all northern peoples of Scandinavia and northern Germany. In the second half of the ninth century, northern Europe was inhabited mainly by various Germanic tribes and the Empire of Charlemagne was divided into three parts.

Different archangelic beings, folk spirits, joined together and in common consultations, in conversing and acting together, the leading being found the best possible arrangements for Christianising Europe. It was then that the archangel of the Roman people joined together with the archangel of the Greeks.

All this is reflected on the plane of historic events and intellectual ideas in the problem faced in the ninth century by Pope Nicholas I (858–867). He was the greatest Pope between Gregory I (590–604) and Gregory VII (1073–1085). He was faced with the problem of how to establish a Christianity that was no longer disturbed by the dying clairvoyant consciousness. He sought to establish a Christianity that in the coming millennium could be taken hold of intellectually; that people could understand the truth of Christianity, at least in a dogmatic sense, for they should think the truth! There was nothing left anymore of the eastern and western mystery knowledge. Nicholas I created exoteric Christianity, that meant an intellectual Christianity started to rule, streaming out of Rome. After Nicholas' death the Council of Constantinople declared that the human being consists only of body and soul, with a few spiritual qualities. With this the cultural decay of the future was predetermined. (The individuality of Nicholas I was reincarnated in the nineteenth century as Field Marshal Helmuth von Moltke who became important for the nineteenth and twentieth centuries, and was a friend of Rudolf Steiner's.)

In the ninth century, while the unknown Parsifal walked through Europe, Nicholas the Great was guided by that great archangel who had the task of directing the exoteric stream of Christianity. Parsifal, on the other hand, was led by the archangel of esoteric Christianity.

The history of the tenth, eleventh, and twelfth centuries led to the flowering of the Middle Ages. In the tenth century there was a renewal of Greek culture within exoteric Christianity, and in Chartres a rebirth of all the wisdom of Plato took place. The teachers of Chartres Platonised Aristotelianism, which also showed itself in the north of Germany through the dramas and poetry of the remarkable woman Hrotsvitha (Roswitha) of Gandersheim.

The events around the Walk of Canossa at that time also show the strengthening and unfolding of exoteric Christianity. Pope Gregory VII in his reforms asserted certain rights over monarchs. The Holy Roman Emperor Henry IV, King of the Germans, disregarded these papal edicts. As a result he was excommunicated by Gregory, whereupon Henry declared the Pope deposed. Henry moved to Italy while Gregory started towards Germany, each to enforce their decrees. On hearing of Henry's arrival Gregory took refuge in the castle of Canossa belonging to Matilda of Tuscany. Matilda, connected to both Henry and Gregory, was a powerful and influential personality who stood behind the curtain of the outer events and silently kept the equilibrium between both. Henry IV took the surprising step of walking to the castle, performing penance and asking the Pope to lift his excommunication. After three days standing in the snow outside the gates of the castle, the Pope rescinded the sentence.[1]

Behind the dominant stream of exoteric Christianity stood the stream of Parsifal, and signs and steps of that stream of Parsifal can be recognised. In Europe the idea arose to go to the east, to save the Holy Sepulchre from the hands of the Muslims. Crusaders, from the nobles to the lowliest, were called and journeyed from Europe to the Holy Land. In essence they longed to find the mysteries of Christianity, which had been suppressed by Pope Nicholas I. The innate longing of the crusaders was esoteric, only their actions were of exoteric nature. In a sense one could say that when they reached the grave, they found it empty. They did not find the Risen Christ, nor did they find the Holy Grail, for which in their innermost being they were searching.

In Jerusalem gradually a kingdom grew. The kings became the outer guardians of the inner longing to find reality. Baldwin IV of Jerusalem lost the flowering of the Knights Templar. The siege took place near the spot where the feeding of the five thousand had taken place at the Sea of Galilee. Between 1185 and 1220 the worst and most evil forces of the enemies of the Holy Grail were assembled: the crusades against Europe, which exterminated everything that was alive from the Grail stream in the north of Spain, the north of Italy and the south of France, in the Cathars and Albigensians. The Holy Grail is at times only spiritual history, at other times touches the ground of the earth.

The whole of Europe had to go a very special way inwardly, although not historically. Behind historical events the evolution of the human soul is hidden. Europe was repeating what had been prepared in the third and fourth post-Atlantean epochs.

What had been prepared in humanity during the Egyptian, the third post-Atlantean epoch, as the sentient soul could instinctively turn towards the spiritual world and behold the spirit and be revived by those forces. We see this depicted in King Arthur and his Knights, reflecting the twelve constellations of the zodiac.

During the fourth post-Atlantean epoch, the Greek people developed the mind soul. Doubt begins to work in the human soul through the wound caused by intellectualism. In the legend of the Holy Grail we find this development represented in Amfortas's wound – the wound which intellectuality inflicts

110

on the human soul. Into this wound fall the dark powers of Klingsor, as the doors to the mysteries are closed.

The fifth post-Atlantean epoch, the European epoch, which has the task to develop the consciousness soul, is also already indicated in the legend of Parsifal. In Parsifal himself, through his quest for the castle of the Holy Grail, the consciousness soul is first hinted at. Parsifal wandered in the guise of fool's clothing, seeking for the old mysteries.

Within the tremendous spectrum of history, various streams and various expressions of yearning arose, and special human beings began to develop the consciousness soul. The path to the Holy Grail must be found today. This path is developing the consciousness soul, the seeking for spirit light that needs to shine into our own existence and lighten our darkness.

2

The Holy Grail and the Consciousness Soul

Lecture 1,
Thursday, April 8, 1954

The development of the west, of Europe, is not only the history of humanity, but the history of evolution itself, the history of the gods. At the turning point of time, particular archangelic beings handed over their tasks to other spiritual beings; others renounced their ascent to higher tasks thereby becoming the leaders of exoteric and esoteric Christianity. Out of these two streams Europe was built. All that took place in Europe itself happened in order to bring about what can be called the Holy Grail. Looking back in history we can discern particular impulses that suddenly appeared without any historical preparatory events or harbingers. Such a thing appeared suddenly in the twelfth and thirteenth centuries with the legend of the Holy Grail. Before this time people had not heard anything of it. In an exoteric way certain legends were told.

There was once a knight Parsifal. His mother was Herzeloyde, his father had been killed by other knights, and he was brought up in loneliness as kind of simpleton or fool. He grew up as an unspoilt human soul. One day per chance he met some knights and thought they were gods. So he went out into the world to become a knight, and his mother died of grief. After many trials, struggles and errors, he came to the castle of the Holy Grail. There he failed to ask what it was and had to leave again. In that very moment, he realised that out of his foolishness, his lack of initiative and interest, he had missed a great moment. So he had to undergo many trials, and in leaving the castle he saw an image in the forest, a young woman, Sigune, was sitting, holding the corpse of her slain bridegroom Schionatulander. This image made a deep impression on his soul, permeating right into the depths of his being. He then accomplished some important deeds and in the end was permitted to return to the castle of the Holy Grail. There he was told that his name had appeared on the Holy Vessel to be the king of the castle.

Soon after such stories emanated a new image appeared in art in France and Germany: the *Vesperbild* or Pietà, certain pictures of the Pietà, going back to the mystics. Thousands of such depictions of the suffering mother Mary were created. This image had to be imprinted into the soul of the people of Europe as it had been into Parsifal's soul. In the ninth century this image was imprinted in Parsifal's soul, as a single human being. Through the working of the leading spiritual beings of the times, three or four hundred years later, tens of thousands of human beings were to meet this picture in order to develop something of the qualities of the Pietà. To this day the most wonderful artistic representation remains Michelangelo's Pietà in St Peter's Basilica in Rome (Plate 10). This Pietà led to the background of the Holy Grail being revealed, for when Rudolf Steiner was trying to understand the Holy Grail the image became alive in him only after he had seen Michelangelo's Pietà.[1]

What is the mystery of the Holy Grail? The human astral body contains the mystery of the Holy Grail. What since olden times in mystery centres was known, and Rudolf Steiner has since openly described, as the astral body, is intimately connected with the Holy Grail. Long ago, human beings were not yet individual, but were part of the ocean of spirit existence surrounding the earth. Distributed over the earth were physical and etheric beings, to which the ocean being of the soul spirit came nearer, leaving drops that became the seeds of single entities that could gradually permeate these physical-etheric bodies. All these single bodies were gradually permeated with this astrality, and became individualised and able to receive an individuality, an 'I'. But there was still a oneness with the divine, a connection to the supersensible. There was no boundary between these individuals and the spiritual world. The astrality was still at one with the higher beings.

This is entirely different from today. At that time we looked down onto our bodies, gradually starting to know that this is *I*. Gradually there came about the will to sacrifice the oneness with the gods, to leave Paradise, in order to become a true self-knowing being. Through this the Fall came about. The gradual recovering from the Fall took a very long time. In Atlantean times this recovery was interrupted, and only after the flood, when in the fourth post-Atlantean epoch, humankind started to migrate from east to west, from India into Europe did they undertake steps to enable our astral body to reunite with the divine. What had condensed out of the ocean of the spirit soul gradually unfolded enabling a reunification. The etheric body developed especially in the ancient Indian epoch, the sentient body in the ancient Persian epoch, the sentient soul unfolded in the Babylonian-Egyptian epoch and the mind soul developed in the Greco-Roman times.

All these steps are like the unfolding of a plant, that leads to the development of the flower. In ancient Indian times the seed of the astral body took root in the etheric body and gradually developed until the time of Europe in the fifth century. The plant of the human astral body had unfolded as far as the crown of its development as flower. In occult language this is called

the *Son of Man,* which signifies the consciousness soul. This is
the seed of manas, buddhi and atman, the still to be developed
higher parts of the human being. The mystery of the Holy Grail
is a mystery of the human astral body.

Going to sleep we expand with our astral body into the astral
ocean in order to clean and heal our astral existence with the
help of spiritual beings. Throughout the centuries this was
developed, and can be compared to a plant growing into the
form of a cup, into a vessel. This empty chalice of our astral
body can, if willing, receive the Son of God, the highest form of
spiritual existence. Through the guiding spiritual beings up as
far as the Archai, we have developed out astral body to this stage.
As Christmas is connected with the ether body, Easter can only
be understood in connection with the astral body. The sting of
the Fall went right into the astral body and only through this can
we develop. The whole of the nervous system permeating us is
the path of our astral body. Rudolf Steiner described the astral
body in sleep:

> Just as the brain, resting within the skull, may be seen as
> a symbol, so the human being on earth appears as living
> enchanted in a castle. The human entity appears as a
> being surrounded and imprisoned behind stone walls.
> The symbol of this ... is the skull ... Forces then stream
> upward from the rest of the organism and sustain this
> being imprisoned in the skull, as though in a fortified
> castle. The forces are directed upward; first the force
> comes from the instrument of the human astral body,
> which extends through the organism. Everything that
> inspires and lends strength and energy to the human
> being streams through the nerve fibres. In the earthly
> human being, this is all united and appears as a mighty
> sword we have forged for ourselves on earth. Then the
> blood's forces stream upward. Gradually, we feel them
> and begin to recognise them, and they appear to us as

what actually wounds the 'brain-being' lying in the enchanted castle of the skull. Like a bleeding lance, the forces stream upward in the etheric body toward the earthly human being lying in the enchanted castle of the brain; we realise that we can observe everything allowed to flow toward the noblest part of the brain.

... From one part of the brain – one small, ennobled part of the brain – the etheric body also rejects everything that comes from the plant kingdom, and it tolerates only the mineral extract; there, in the vital part of the brain, this mineral extract is united with the purest and noblest radiance entering through the sense organs. Here, the purest, noblest element in light, sound, and warmth encounters the most refined products of the mineral kingdom. The noblest part of the brain is nourished by the union between the most delicate sense impressions and the most refined mineral products.

... All of this, brought together in pictures gave us the Grail legend.[2]

The astral body was given to human beings in the time of the Old Moon. Dynameis and angels handed astrality over to man. Time and again we can observe in the waxing crescent moon the sign of the sun in it; it is the moon sickle with the patina. In this moon sickle is inscribed: *gangangda greida,* the wandering balm.[3] Steiner described how in the moment he read the stellar script and saw the crescent moon with the disc of the sun in it, and the name Parsifal, inscribed upon it in occult script.[4] This in turn leads him to the image of the Pietà. It is Sigune, Sophia or Mary, holding the body of the son, like the image of the moon that carries the sun in it.

So the images derive from the same source of spirit as the human soul strives for in the search for the castle of the Holy Grail. If the astral body follows its true inborn interest and unites itself with the Grail, it will reach the horizon of general humanity.

The astral body carries in itself the powers of egotism, which in itself is very necessary, but we have to unfold it in such a way that interest in the world and love for the world heal this egotism of our astral body. In Amfortas we perceive a person who carried his personal interests into his deeds; in Parsifal we have a person whose individuality had not yet developed, and only when he started his journeys could his individuality arise in his astral body. Between these two there stands the chalice of the flower, ready to receive the spirit seed. This is possible only where two or three are together 'in my name'. In groups of human beings the chalice of our astrality becomes a vessel for the spirit and for the Christ. This cannot be achieved alone, but only with others.

What happens to the astral body of the human being when it is fully developed on the esoteric path? The astral body becomes like a sun, shining and radiating, and the 'I' or self parts into seven different beings, becoming the planets around the sun of our astral body. One part of our own self, one of the seven planets, is to meet the angels, another one the archangels and the third one the Archai, and so on, so that out of our spirit existence the sevenhood of our self is again instilled into the spirit, like a planetary system. The eighth part then meets with the whole of the zodiac.

In the Book of Revelation there are the letters to the congregations. The fifth one, to Sardis, relates to the fifth post-Atlantean epoch. The seven spirits and the seven stars are what we need to achieve in this epoch. The name Sardis seems to point to the Grail. In that letter we can read:

> You have the name of a living being, yet you are dead.
> Strive to awaken in your consciousness, and strengthen
> what is still living in your soul so that it die not ...
> Therefore revive in your memory all that you have
> received and heard from the spiritual worlds. Care for it
> in your soul, and change your heart and mind.

We need to awake for that which we have carried from the spirit world. Our astral body is imperfect, though is has learnt to be watchful. Then the letter continues:

> He who overcomes shall also be clothed in white, and I will not blot out his name from the Book of Life.[5]

Those in the white garments can be called Parsifals, to whom the doors are open.

This is where we meet the mystery of the Holy Grail, which is also the task of our times. Sardis is the whole of Europe, the representative of the fifth post-Atlantean epoch. To receive the white garment is to fill the empty chalice with the consciousness soul, with the first drops of dew of the spirit that the being of Anthroposophia can give to us. This is what should be carried into the Easter festival.

Appendix

The facsimiles and English translations of documents from the Karl König Archive show aspects described in the Introduction or related to König's lectures.

They include examples from Karl König's lecture notes in the early years, notes from the 1940s, at the beginning of the building period in Camphill, when König was especially occupied with the connection between St John and the Grail, and diary entries from the period in which the lectures in this book were given.

The experience of the yearly festivals in the human body

From the manuscript of a lecture that Karl König gave at the Goetheanum, May 21, 1929.

The third system is the nervous system. We will take the brain as the most characteristic. In observing this brain, we notice the wonderful symmetry that is there. Nowhere do we find such symmetry as in our brain. The right and left coils appear in an endless symmetry; there is a connection there – called the bridge. And when we ask what informs and underlies it, we can experience how the brain determines right and left.

As Parsifal approached the Grail castle, Gurnemanz said to him: 'My son, here time becomes space.' And Parsifal stands astounded, not understanding why Gurnemanz says this. But these words are true for the Grail castle, and just as true for our brain. We cannot understand its structure until we realise that in it, time has become space.

Scientists say that these coils and convolutions and loops are formed this way in order to create room for endless material in a small space. This is also true, but it is time – that which was spread out in the etheric world – that is drawn into the prison cell of our skull and formed into the brain.

Vortrag Goetheanum 4. Oktober 1930
(at The Michaelmas Conference)
(Polarity: senses and The thinking ... the human face and The 4 seasons and Archangels)

I 1) Goethes Begegnung mit Schillers Schädel.

Schaun Gefäß, Orakelsprüche spendend,
Wie bin ich wert, dich in der Hand zu halten?
Was kann der Mensch im Leben mehr gewinnen,
Als daß sich Gott-Natur ihm offenbare!
Wie sie das Feste läßt zu Geist verrinnen,
Wie sie das Geistgefügte fest bewahre!

   2) An der Gestalt des Hauptes erlebt Goethe diese Worte.
Das Haupt ist etwas Besonderes an uns. Es ist hinauf-
gehoben in die Welt, entrückt der Erde.

   3) Das Haupt stellt die <u>Sinnes- Denkorganisation</u> dar.
Die Sinne kommen von außen.   Blut; Nerven
Die Denkorganisation von oben. (28. III. 1925)
Das ist die Teilung in Schirm- & Gesichtsschädel.
Mensch & Welt bauen am Haupte.

   4) Das Erlebnis des Hauptes: Es ist nicht Da, es ist reines
Opfer.

II 1) Die Gliederung des Gesichtes. Vier Sinnesorgane &
alle vier sind dennoch Eines. Das gleiche Urbild
wirkt in ihnen.
Aus <u>Aktion</u> & <u>Rezeption</u> sind sie gebildet.
Blut & Nerv treten in ihnen zusammen.

Die vier Bildekräfte wirken in ihnen   Ohr: Wärme
                                          Auge: Licht
                                          Mund: Klang
                                          Nase: Leben.

   2) Aus je zweien formiert sich die
Form der Schalsschale

122

Lecture, Goetheanum, October 4, 1930

(at the Michaelmas Conference)
(Polarity of senses and the thinking; the human face and the 4 seasons and archangels)

I 1) Goethe's encounter with Schiller's skull.
Mysterious vessel that speaks as oracle,
To hold you in my hand I am most humbled.
O what more in life can human beings gain
Than that to us the divine may reveal!
How spirit fruits in substance fast remain,
How substance over time to spirit yields!

2) Goethe experiences these words in observing the form of the head.
The head is a special part of us. It is raised up into the world, away from the earth.

3) The head represents the <u>sensing-thinking organisation.</u>
The <u>senses</u> come from outside. Blood and nerve.
The <u>thinking organisation</u> from above. (22. III. 1925)
This is the division of brain & skull.
Human beings and the world form out the head.

4) The experience of the head: it is not there; it is pure sacrifice.

II 1) The structure of the face. Four sense organs & all four are also as one. The same archetype is active in them.
They are formed by <u>activity</u> and <u>receptivity.</u>
Blood and nerve meet in them.
The four formative forces are active in them
  ear: warmth
  eye: light
  mouth: sound
  nose: life

2) Out of each pair is formed
The shape of the Grail chalice

31)   Die xristliche Substanz der Welt
                Der Gral,
        Das ist das Zusammenspiel von
            Sonne, Mond & Erde.
        Der mit seinen Sinnen & damit
        mit seinem Kopf nach aussen
        gewendete Mensch, er muss in
        seinem Herzen
                    Den Glauben
        tragen.
        Der mit seinem Willen nach
        innen gewendete Mensch, der
        Offenbarung hingegeben, er
        muss in seinen Gliedern
                    die Hoffnung
        tragen.
            Der Glaube ist dem Monde zugewandt.
        Deshalb wandelt der Glaube, wird klein
            oder gross, hell oder Dunkel.
        Der Glaube ist ein Kind der Nacht.
            Die Hoffnung ist der Sonne zugewandt.
        Deshalb ist die Hoffnung Da oder nicht da;
            ist stark oder schwach, hoch oder tief.

Six pages from König's journal of 1940 while interned on the Isle of Man.

31)   The Christ substance of the Grail world
Is the interplay of sun, moon & earth.
The human being turned outward
With the senses and thereby with the head,
Must bear
<u>Faith</u>
In the heart.

The human being turned inward
With his will, surrendered to the revelation,
Must bear
<u>Hope</u>
In his limbs.

Faith turns toward the moon.
Therefore, faith changes:
Grows small or large, light or dark.
Faith is a child of night.
Hope turns toward the sun.
Therefore, hope is either there or not there,
Is strong or weak, high or low.

Die Hoffnung ist ein Kind des Tages.
So wandert der Glaube,
Die Hoffnung aber besteht.
Von der Geburt kommen wir,
Und blicken glaubend auf sie zurück.
Zum Tode gehen wir hin
Und schauen hoffend zu ihm hinauf.
Denn der Mond ist das Tor der Geburt
Und die Sonne die Pforte des Todes.
Vom Mondensein kommen wir,
Ins Sonnensein gehen wir.
Der Glaube tönt +
Die Hoffnung leuchtet.
Aus der Mutter kommen wir
+ zum Vater gehen wir.
Aber Xristus sprach:
  „Niemand kommt zum Vater denn durch mich."
Ich kann an Jesus glauben
+ darf auf Xristus hoffen.
Ich kann Glaubenslieder singen,
Um Jesus zu bekennen.
Und Hoffnungslicht in mir entzünden
Um Xristi Geist in mir zu beleben

21

Hope is a child of day.
So faith changes,
But hope remains.
We come from birth,
And look <u>faithfully</u> back at it.
We go toward death
And look <u>hopefully</u> up to it.
For the moon is the gateway of birth
And the sun the portal of death.
We come from moon existence;
We go into sun existence.
Faith sounds &
Hope shines.
We come from the mother
& go to the father.
But Christ spoke:
'No one comes to the Father but through me.'
I can have faith in Jesus
& may hope for the Christ.
I can sing songs of faith,
To praise Jesus.
And kindle the light of hope in myself
To enliven the spirit of Christ in me.

Den Kristus - Jesus aber,
Wie find ich ihn?
Wenn Glaube & Hoffnung ineinander strömen,
Wenn Mond & Sonne einander begegnen,
Dann wird der Glaube Demütig,
Und der Mond wird zur Schale,
Dann wird die ~~Hoffnung~~milde
Und die Sonne wird zur Scheibe.
Wird aber der Glaubens - Mond
zur Schale, dann ist er
     Frommsein.
Wird die Sonnen - Hoffnung
zur Scheibe, dann ist sie
     Liebe.
Die Liebes - Scheibe
    in der
Frommheits - Schale
    Das ist
    der
    Gral.

       ✠   (24. IX. 1940)

But how can I find
Jesus Christ?
When faith & hope stream together,
When moon & sun meet each other,
Then faith will become humble
And the moon a chalice;
Then hope will become gentle
And the sun a disc.
If the moon of faith becomes a chalice,
It will be
<u>Piety.</u>
If the sun of hope becomes a disc,
It will be
<u>Love.</u>
The love-disc
In the
Piety-chalice:
This is
The
<u>Grail.</u>

(24. IX. 1940)

Monden - Glaubens - Schale
    Trägerin
Der Weins der Frommheit.

Sonnen - Hoffnungs - Scheibe
    Spenderin
Der Brot's des Liebe

    Gral des Alls
    Erwärme Du
mit Deinem Wein das Herz
    Erleuchte Du
mit Deinem Brot das Haupt
    unseres Daseins,
    damit
    Xristi Wesen
    in uns
    walten kann.

    ✠   (28. IX. 1940)

Moon-faith-chalice:
Bearer
Of the wine of piety

Sun-hope-disc:
Giver
Of the bread of love

Grail of all,
Warm
With your wine the heart,
Enlighten
With your bread the mind
Of our existence,
So that
The being of Christ
Can rule
In us.

(28. IX. 1940)

33.)
Das Gehirn ist der Glaube.
Der Stoffwechsel ist die Hoffnung,
Das Herz aber ist das Frommsein.

—

Elias - Johannes führen den Glauben,
leiten zu Jesus.
Johannes ist der Glaube.

Johannes - Novalis leiten zur Hoffnung,
führen zu Kristus.
Johannes ist die Hoffnung.

Jesus ist Frommsein,
Kristus ist Liebe.

Für den Kristus, der in der Gestalt
der Taube erscheint,
Opfert Johannes sein Haupt.

Für Jesus, der in Gestalt
des Lammes erscheint,
Opfert Lazarus seinen Leib.

33)   The brain is faith,
The metabolism is hope
But the heart is piety.
—

Elijah-John to guide our faith,
To lead us to Jesus.
John is faith.

John-Novalis to lead us to hope,
To guide us to Christ.
John is hope.

Jesus is piety,
Christ is love.

For the Christ, who appears
In the form of the dove,
John sacrifices his head.

For Jesus, who appears
In the form of the lamb,
Lazarus sacrifices his body.

Der Xristus erweckt den Leib
Des Lazarus,
Der Jesus übernimmt den Kopf
Des Johannes.

So ist Lazarus – Johannes
Der Gral.

⚕

34.)

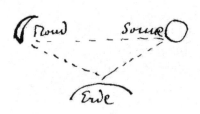

Dieses Zusammenspiel erfolgt aus der
Substanz der Liebe.
  Opfer ist Sonnenweggang.
  Opfer ist Mondenaustritt.
  Opfer ist Erdenhingabe.

⚕

The Christ awakens the body
Of Lazarus.
Jesus takes up the head
Of John.

So Lazarus-John
Is the Grail.

34)

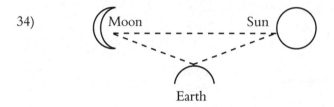

This interplay comes from the substance of love.

Sacrifice is the departure of the sun.
Sacrifice is the exit of the moon.
Sacrifice is the surrender of the earth.

Goetheanum

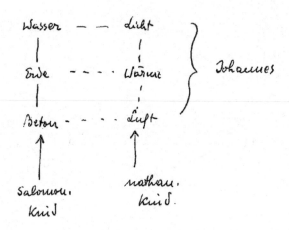

Tierwesen : Frage
Pflanzen : Antwort.

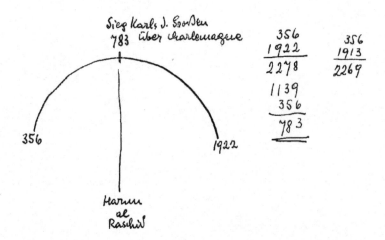

Four pages from preparation work for the 'Double Conference' in 1945 in Camphill Aberdeen (first the physicians' conference, then the conference on Goethe and the arts).

<u>Goetheanum</u>

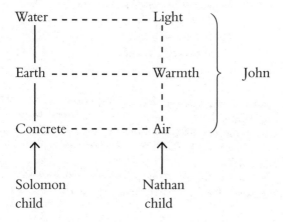

Animals: question
Plants: answer

Victory of Charles the Great over Charlemagne★

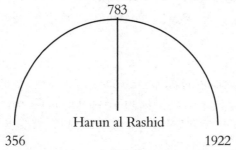

★ An error as they are two names of the same person. It should probably have read *Victory of Charlemagne over Saxony*

137

Schaue den Logos
Im sengenden Feuer
Finde die Lösung
In Dianens Haus.

Behold the Logos
In the searing fire,
Find the solution
In Diana's temple.

Now there stood by the cross of Jesus his mother, & his mother's sister, Mary the wife of Cleophas & Mary Magdalene.
When Jesus therefore saw his mother, & the disciple standing by, whom he loved, he saith unto his mother, Woman, behold thy son!
Then saith he to the disciple, Behold thy mother! And from that hour that disciple took her unto his own home!

"Jesus saith unto him, If I will that he tarry till I come, what is that to thee?

Vorüber ging der lange Traum der Schmerzen
Sophie ist ewig Priesterin der Herzen.

Translation of the last two lines:
The long-drawn dream of pain is finally over
Sophie is priestess of our hearts forever.

Die Erfüllung des ägyptischen Mysterien im Auftauchen des Grales!

*Christus Wollen
Im Menschen wirkend
Es wird Lucifer entreißen
Und auf des Geistes Wissens Booten
In Menschenseelen auferwecken
Isis-Sophia,
Des Gottes Weisheit.*

———

The fulfilment of the Egyptian mysteries in the emergence of the Grail!

The will of Christ
Works in humanity
From Lucifer will be taken
And on the boats of spirit knowledge
Re-awakened in human souls
Isis-Sophia,
The wisdom of God.

Goethe & Schiller,

Sie bilden etwas wie ein geistiges Goetheanum.

Schiller: die kleine Kuppel

Goethe: die große Kuppel

Schiller	Goethe
das	das
Gewissen	Gedächtnis
Elias	Moses

Beide
bilden
das Bild der
Verklärung.
Zwischen ihnen
erscheint die Anthroposophie.

Gespräch zwischen Schiller & Goethe: 20. Juli 1794
                                          + 32 $\frac{1}{3}$

Auftrag für eine gemeinsame Gruft
    von Goethe & Schiller.   November 1826
                                          + 32 $\frac{1}{3}$
"Im ernsten Beinhaus wars".!!   März 1859
                                          + 32 $\frac{1}{3}$
        Rudolf Steiner geht nach Weimar Juli 1890
                                          + 32 $\frac{1}{3}$
        ~~Goetheanum~~ Weihnachtstagung
        ~~brennt nieder~~!   November 1923

Goethe & Schiller,
They form something like a spiritual Goetheanum.
Schiller: the small dome
Goethe: the large dome

Schiller   Goethe
<u>Conscience</u>   <u>Memory</u>
Elijah   Moses
both
form
the image of the
Transfiguration.
Between them
anthroposophy appears.

Conversation between Schiller & Goethe: July 20, 1794

Request for a shared tomb   November, 1826
for Goethe and Schiller.
'It was in the gloomy burial vault'!!   March, 1859

Rudolf Steiner goes to Weimar   July, 1891

Christmas conference   November, 1923

Aus dem Zyklus „Alte Mythen & ihre Bedeutung",
sind die folgenden Worte besonders bedeutungsvoll:
(S. 164) „Wird man sich herzenswarme Vorstellungen
machen können darüber, daß wenn man hinschaut
auf das menschliche Haupt, man in dem mensch-
lichen Haupte ein Abbild des ganzen sternbesäten
Weltenraumes mit seinen Wundern sieht, dann werden in die menschliche Seele hereinkommen alle
Bilder über den Zusammenhang des Menschen mit
dem weiten, weiten Weltenall. Und diese Bilder
werden zu Erzählungsformen, die wir heute noch
nicht haben. und diese Erzählungsformen werden
nicht abstrakt, aber empfindungsmäßig zum Ausdruck bringen dasjenige, was wir in die Herzen der
jüngsten Kinder gießen können, so daß diese Herzen der jüngsten Kinder empfinden: hier auf der
Erde stehe ich als Mensch, aber als Mensch bin ich
ein Ausdruck des ganzen, sternbesäten Weltenraumes: in mir spricht sich aus die ganze Welt.' ——

Diese Worte hängen damit zusammen, daß Er-
zählungen um den heiligen Gral & Parzifal erste-
hen werden, die geschaffen sind aus der tiefen Ver-
senkung in den Bau des Gehirns & die Form un-
seres Hauptes.

ↄ

From König's notebook, 1942

In the cycle *Ancient Myths & Their Meaning,* the following words are especially significant: (p. 164) 'If we can warm-heartedly imagine that when we look at the human head we see in it an image of the whole star-strewn cosmos with its wonders, then all images of the human connection to the wide, wide cosmos will arise in the human soul. And these images become story forms that we do not yet have today; and these story forms will express – not abstractly, but with feeling – that which we can pour into the hearts of the youngest children so that these youngest children's hearts feel: here on earth I am a human being, but as a human being I am an expression of the whole star-strewn cosmos: in me, the whole world speaks out.'

These words are connected to stories of the Holy Grail and Parsifal that will arise, which are created from the deep immersion in the formation of the brain & the form of our head.

Das alles erweiterte sich zu dem Aufbau-Bild des Evangeliums in folgender Weise:

Im 1. Kapitel wird das Geheimnis der Erdensphäre ausgesprochen: Die Fleisch-Erd-Werdung des Wortes. Und dieses erste Kapitel, als die Ouverture des Gesamt-Werkes umschließt viele Geheimnisse. Es ist separiert von den übrigen Kapiteln. Ein Ganzes in sich selbst gleich dem letzten Kapitel. Das 1. und das 21. Kapitel stehen wie zwei Säulen um die übrigen 19 Kapitel, die gleich einem Tor sind.

Auf diesem Tor steht geschrieben:

"Ich bin die Tür".

Und vor der Türe steht

"Der gute Hirte".

Neunzehn Kapitel hat das Buch (12 + 7), wie die Klassenstunden neunzehn sind an der Zahl, wie die Säulen am Tempel zu Ephesus neunzehn an der Langseite waren.

18

144

Notes for Pentecost 1943

This all extended to the image of the structure of [St John's] Gospel as follows.

In the first chapter, the mystery of the earthly sphere is spoken: the flesh-earth-becoming of the word. And this first chapter, as overture to the whole work, contains many mysteries. It is separate from the other chapters. A whole unto itself, like the last chapter. The 1st and the 21st chapters stand like two pillars containing the remaining 19 chapters, like a gate.

On this gate is written:
'I am the doorway.'

And before the doorway is written:
'The Good Shepherd.'

The Book has nineteen chapters (12 + 7), as there are nineteen class lessons [of the School of Spiritual Science], as there were nineteen pillars on the long side of the Temple of Ephesus.

Liest man die Anfangsverse des ersten Kapitels, dann erstrahlen sie gleich einer Sonnenscheibe bis zu den Worten:

„Und das Licht scheint
In der Finsternis;
Aber die Finsternis
Hat's nicht begriffen."

Und dann plötzlich, zaghaft, voll Menschlichkeit & voll Leid ertönt es:

„Es ward ein Mensch,
Gesandt war er von Gott.
Der hieß Johannes".

Wie eine Schale formen sich diese Worte & bilden den Kelch, der das vorher besungene Licht trägt. Und schon wird gesagt:

„Er war nicht das Licht,
Sondern daß er zeugte
Von dem Licht".

Das ist das Bild des Grals:

69.

146

Notes for Pentecost 1943

If we read the beginning verses of the first chapter, they blaze like a disc of sun toward the words:

> 'And the light shone
> in the darkness;
> but the darkness
> comprehended it not.'

And then suddenly, tentatively, full of humanity & full of suffering, sound the words:

> 'A human being
> was sent from God,
> who was called John.'

Like a bowl, these words form and create the chalice that bears the light praised before. And it is said:

> 'He was not the light,
> but bore witness
> to the light.'

This is the image of the Grail:

> In the beginning was the Word
> A human being was.

Tuesday May 5

Morgens denke ich viel an die Zeit von vor 24 Jahren. Die Hochzeit & die erste Zeit der Ehe. Dann schaue ich das Hochzeits-Horoskop an & bin erschüttert zu sehen, daß im Augenblick der Trauung, der Mond durch den 23. Grad Jungfrau hindurch geht, der Grad, in welchem viele Grals-ereignisse sich vollziehen, auch die Grund-steinlegung des Goetheanums, der Brand & der erste Bibelabend im August 1941. So ist das also vorgezeichnet. Außerdem aber ist Jupiter im aufsteigenden Mond-Knoten & das ist wahrscheinlich die Indi-kation dafür, daß um Tilla & mich die ganze Community sich herumformiert hat. Daß diese Ehe zu einem Kristalli-sationspunkt von so vielen Menschen-schicksalen geworden ist & zum Zentral-punkt sozialer Strukturen.

From König's diary, 1953

In the morning, I think a lot about the time 24 years ago. The wedding & the first years of marriage. Then I look at the wedding horoscope & am astonished to see that at the moment of the vows, the moon is going through the 23rd degree of Virgo; the degree at which many Grail events take place, also the foundation stone laying of the Goetheanum, the fire & the first Bible evening in 1941. Thus it is presaged. In addition, Jupiter is in the ascending moon node, & that is probably the indication for the whole community forming around Tilla & me. For this marriage becoming a crystallisation point for so many human destinies & the central point of social structures.

Excerpt from König's diary, written after the lecture on Thursday, April 1, 1954

This morning, the clinic is in Heathcot and several insights arise regarding the problem of movement disorders. The difference between extra-pyramidal and pyramidal is clear.

After a few other things this afternoon, I try to prepare for the second lecture on the Grail. I read some things that Rudolf Steiner said on the subject, but it is only when I take up the lecture from the folk soul cycle, in which it is explained how single archangelic beings take over higher tasks through renunciation, that I find my starting point. The archangel of the Greeks becomes the leader of exoteric, and the archangel of the Celts becomes leader of esoteric Christianity. Now I see how the whole history of Europe becomes the exterior—the raiment—of the 'Holy Grail'; how human beings are only parts of the stories of the gods and how these take place in order to bring human beings to higher development.

I try to explain this, but succeed only very partially, and afterwards I am very depressed by my failure.

From König's diary, Sunday, February 25, 1962

This morning I am putting together the lecture list of Rudolf Steiner's statements on the topic of 'Paul and the Holy Grail'. In the process, I stumble across very important information in the second lecture, 'The Philosophy of Thomas Aquinas.' The School of Athens is coming increasingly to the fore.

... [Some parts of this diary missing; there is only an incomplete transcript for this year and no original]

Then I prepare myself for the evening's lecture. It is on Dionysius the Areopagite. [I am] reading a lot about the Eleusinian mysteries and about ancient world wisdom. The lecture itself is a very special experience for the audience. They are all deeply moved, though I myself do not know why it was so special.

From preparatory notes for a lecture in 1960 about the Goetheanum

> He who failed in Egypt
>> the young man of Sais.
> Was awakened through Christ
>> the young man of Nain.
> Achieved the Grail
>> as Parsifal.

Notes

In some quotations spelling and capitalisation has been amended.

Introduction

1 Steiner, *An Outline of Esoteric Science,* p. 388.
2 Unpublished paper, KKA, Aberdeen.
3 Unpublished paper, KKA, Aberdeen.
4 Heyer, *Kaspar Hauser.* König's book review is reprinted in *Kaspar Hauser and Karl König,* pp. 147–51.

St Paul and the Grail

1 The School of Athens

1 Lecture of Dec 26, 1961 (one of seven lectures on conscience, Newton Dee, Dec 3, 1961 – Jan 12, 1962, unpublished MS, KKA).
2 Steiner, *Between Death and Rebirth,* lecture of Dec 22, 1912. König's copy has many underlinings and notes, showing how much he worked on this subject.
3 Steiner, 'Raffaels Mission im Lichte der Wissenschaft vom Geiste,' lecture of Jan 30, 1913 in *Ergebnisse der Geistesforschung.*
4 Lecture of May 6, 1912, last published in German in *Das Goetheanum,* March–April 1937 (Vol.16, Nos. 12–16).
5 Steiner, *Art History as a Reflection of Inner Spiritual Impulses,* lecture of Oct 5, 1917, p. 251.
6 Steiner, *Art History as a Reflection of Inner Spiritual Impulses,* lecture of Nov 1, 1916, p. 66f.
7 Fischel, *Raphael.* Fischel died in 1939 trying to flee Nazi Germany. His book was only published in the original German in 1962 in Berlin.
8 Fischel quotes this sonnet in *Raphaels Zeichnungen.* It begins with the lines: *Come non pode dir d'arcana dei / Paul come discesofu dal celo /Cose el mio cor d'uno amoroso velo / A ricoperto tuti i penso mei.*
9 Steiner, *Art History as a Reflection of Inner Spiritual Impulses,* lecture of Oct 5, 1917, p. 246.

2 The Mithras Mysteries, Eleusis and the Rosicrucians

1 This and the following quotes from *The Spiritual Hierarchies and the Physical World,* lecture of April 12 morning, 1909, pp. 13–15.

2 *Original Impulses for the Science of the Spirit,* lecture of March 25, 1907, pp. 234.

3 This is a fairly free paraphrasing by König, probably from *Divine Names,* 5.3.

4 *Materialism and the Task of Anthroposophy,* lecture of June 2, 1921, p. 278.

5 *Rosicrucian Wisdom,* lecture of June 6, 1907, p. 154.

3 The Sixth Century

1 *The Spiritual Hierarchies and the Physical World,* lecture of April 12 morning, 1909, pp. 13f.

2 New Testament translation by Jon Madsen.

3 *The Redemption of Thinking,* lecture of May 23, 1920, p. 63.

4 This and the following quote from *Materialism and the Task of Anthroposophy,* lecture of April 15, 1921, pp. 63f.

4 Central Europe, Threefolding and the Grail

1 *Materialism and the Task of Anthroposophy,* lecture of April 16, 1920, pp. 79f.

2 This and the following quote from *Materialism and the Task of Anthroposophy,* lecture of April 16, 1920, pp. 80f.

5 The Path of Wisdom through History

1 This and the following quotes from *The Spiritual Hierarchies and the Physical World,* lecture of April 12 morning, 1909, pp. 5–7.

2 This and the following quote from *Festivals and their Meaning,* lecture of April 3, 1920, p. 143–145.

3 *Christ and the Spiritual World,* lecture of Jan 1, 1914, p. 97.

4 *The East in the Light of the West,* lecture of Aug 23, 1909, p. 4.

5 *The East in the Light of the West,* lecture of Aug 31, 1909, pp. 213f, 215.

6 King Arthur and the New Organ of Conscience

1 *Festivals and their Meaning,* lecture of April 3, 1920, p. 144.

2 Half a year earlier, in September 1961 König had given three lectures on memory and continued the series in December and January 1962 about conscience. He often spoke about these as being themes on many journeys at that time, and they also played part in the naming of the Camphill Hall that was just being built (see *Becoming Human: A Social Task,* pp. 38ff, and *Kaspar Hauser and Karl König,* pp. 127ff).

3 *The Effects of Esoteric Development,* lecture of March 25, 1913, pp. 129f.
4 *Theosophy,* pp. 45f.
5 *Mysteries of the East and of Christianity,* lecture of Feb 7, 1913, p. 61.
6 Novalis, *Henry von Ofterdingen,* p. 164.

7 Three Stages of Conscience

1 *Christ and the Spiritual World,* lecture of Jan 1, 1914, pp. 109f.
2 In September 1961 König had given three lectures on memory
   and continued the series in December and January 1962 about
   conscience.
3 *Universal Spirituality and Human Physicality.*
4 *The Christ Impulse,* lecture of May 8, 1910, p. 129.
5 'The Etherisation of the Blood,' lecture of Oct 1, 1911 in *Esoteric
   Christianity.*

The Holy Grail

1 Exoteric and Esoteric Christianity

1 The background to the Walk of Canossa has been inserted here from
   an unpublished lecture by König that he gave a week earlier on
   March 25, 1954.

2 The Holy Grail and the Consciousness Soul

1 Steiner relates this in *Christ and the Spiritual World,* lecture of Jan 1,
   1914, pp. 99f.
2 *The Effects of Esoteric Development,* lecture of March 25, 1913, pp. 128–30.
3 The expression occurs in thirteenth-century legend of Parsifal written
   in the Nordic language (akin to modern Icelandic). The Grail is
   here called *ganganda greida,* from *gehend,* moving or going about, and
   greida, meaning literally 'things', and in this context indicating balm,
   provisions, or nourishment.
4 *Christ and the Spiritual World,* lecture of Jan 1, 1914, pp. 110f.
5 Rev.3:1–3, 5. New Testament translation by Jon Madsen.

Bibliography

Fischel, Oskar, *Raphael* (tr. Bernard Rackham), London 1948.

—, *Raphaels Zeichnungen*, Berlin 1925.

Heyer, Karl, *Kaspar Hauser und das Schicksal Mitteleuropas im 19. Jahrhundert,* second ed. Stuttgart 1983.

König, Karl, *Kaspar Hauser and Karl König,* Floris Books 2012.

Madsen, Jon (trans.) *The New Testament,* Floris Books 2000.

Novalis, *Henry von Ofterdingen*, (tr. Palmer Hilty) Frederick Ungar, New York 1964.

Steiner, Rudolf. Volume Nos refer to the Collected Works (CW), or to the German Gesamtausgabe (GA).

—, *Art History as a Reflection of Inner Spiritual Impulses* (CW 292), SteinerBooks, USA 2016.

—, *Between Death and Rebirth* (CW 141), Rudolf Steiner Press, UK 1975.

—, *Christ and the Spiritual World and the Search for the Holy Grail* (CW 149), Rudolf Steiner Press, UK 2008.

—, *Christ Impulse and the Development of Ego Consciousness, The* (CW 116), Rudolf Steiner Press, UK 2014.

—, *East in the Light of the West, The* (CW 113), Spiritual Science Library, USA 1986.

—, *The Effects of Esoteric Development* (CW 145), Anthroposophic Press, USA 1997.

—, *Ergebnisse der Geistesforschung* (GA 62), Dornach 1988.

—, *Esoteric Christianity and the Mission of Christian Rosenkreutz* (CW 130), Rudolf Steiner Press, UK 2000.

—, *Intuitive Thinking as a Spiritual Path: A Philosophy of Freedom* (CW 4), Anthroposophic Press, USA 1995 (also published as *The Philosophy of Freedom,* Rudolf Steiner Press, UK 2011).

—, *Materialism and the Task of Anthroposophy* (CW 204), Anthroposophic Press, USA 1987.

—, *Mysteries of the East and of Christianity, The* (CW 144), Rudolf Steiner Press, UK 1972.

—, *Original Impulses for the Science of the Spirit* (CW 96), Completion Press, Australia 2001.

—, *Outline of Esoteric Science, An* (CW 13), Anthroposophic Press, USA 1997.

—, *Philosophy of Freedom, The* (CW 4), Rudolf Steiner Press, UK 2011 (also published as *Intuitive Thinking as a Spiritual Path: A Philosophy of Freedom,* Anthroposophic Press, USA 1995).

—, *Redemption of Thinking: A Study in the Philosophy of Thomas Aquinas, The* (CW 74), Anthroposophic Press, USA 1983.

—, *Rosicrucian Wisdom* (CW 99), Rudolf Steiner Press, UK 2000.

—, *Spiritual Hierarchies and the Physical World: Zodiac, Planets and Cosmos, The* (CW 110), SteinerBooks, USA 2008.

—, *Theosophy* (CW 9), Anthroposophic Press, USA 1994.

—, *Universal Spirituality and Human Physicality: Bridging the Divide* (CW 202), Rudolf Steiner Press, UK 2014.

Index

Karl König's collected works are being published in English by Floris Books and in German by Verlag Freies Geistesleben. They are issued by the Karl König Archive in co-operation with the Ita Wegman Institute for Basic Research into Anthroposophy. They encompass the entire, wide-ranging literary estate of Karl König, including his books, essays, manuscripts, lectures, diaries, notebooks, his extensive correspondence and his artistic works, across twelve subjects.

Karl König Archive subjects

Medicine and study of the human being
Curative education and social therapy
Psychology and education
Agriculture and science
Social questions
The Camphill movement
Christianity and the festivals
Anthroposophy
Spiritual development
History and biographies
Artistic and literary works
Karl König's biography

Karl König Archive
www.karl-koenig-archive.net
kk.archive@camphill.net

Ita Wegman Institute for Basic
Research into Anthroposophy
www.wegmaninstitut.ch
koenigarchiv@wegmaninstitut.ch